Reggie Burrows Hodges   Hawkeye

Reggie Burrows Hodges   Hawkeye

May 28–September 11, 2022

Center for Maine Contemporary Art
Rockland, Maine

CMCA

Foreword

The Center for Maine Contemporary Art (CMCA) is honored to have worked with Reggie Burrows Hodges to premier his first solo museum exhibition, *Hawkeye*, in the summer of 2022. Hodges's contributions to painting have only recently begun to be fully recognized, and this exhibition crystallizes the artist's significance within both Maine's rich arts community and the larger field of contemporary art. The artist is noted for his formal technique of leaving exposed the black hue of his primed canvases to color his figures, while rendering their environments and clothing in vibrant, gestural strokes.

In the works in this exhibition, Hodges explored concepts of memory, loss, time, and trajectory, ultimately focusing on depicting moments from his childhood in the early 1970s in Compton, California. Seven of the twelve paintings in the exhibition capture scenes of daily routines and recreation that remain fixed in the artist's memory, including striking portraits of his parents, *Father's Self-Portrait* (2019) and *Melba 77* (2021). In the years following the loss of his parents, the artist found personal metaphors for parental guidance in sports, specifically Hawk-Eye, the electronic line-calling system used in professional tennis, and referees or umpires in the act of conferring or decision making (see, for example, *Referees: And Then There Were Three*, 2020). In the works that take Hawk-Eye as their subject, Hodges tightens his focus further, honing in on split seconds appropriated from real matches, when the ball's trajectory leaves a shadow where it struck the court's surface, flattened by its speed into a dark, elongated oval. The paintings in this exhibition form a singular body of work within the artist's career to date, offering brief glimpses into defining concepts of family, arbitration, recollection, and the passage of time.

We are profoundly grateful to Reggie Burrows Hodges for entrusting the CMCA with this important exhibition. Our great thanks go to Karma's staff, especially Brendan Dugan, for their support of the exhibition throughout its development and the production of this catalogue. It is important to note that *Reggie Burrows Hodges: Hawkeye* is, in part, the culmination of the artist's receipt of the 2021 Ellis-Beauregard Foundation's prestigious Fellowship in the Visual Arts, which recognizes artistic excellence.

The exhibition was made possible through grants from the Andy Warhol Foundation for the Visual Arts and Ellis-Beauregard Foundation, by the artist's galleries Karma and Dowling Walsh Gallery, and with the additional support of Bank of America Private Bank, Marty Jones & Christine Armstrong, Marilyn Moss Rockefeller and Pamela and James Wise. The exhibition and related programming would not be possible without the tireless work of the CMCA's staff and the support of our non-collecting museum's board of trustees.

Timothy Peterson
Executive Director and Chief Curator
Center for Maine Contemporary Art

Jennifer King
Painting between Knowledge and Feeling

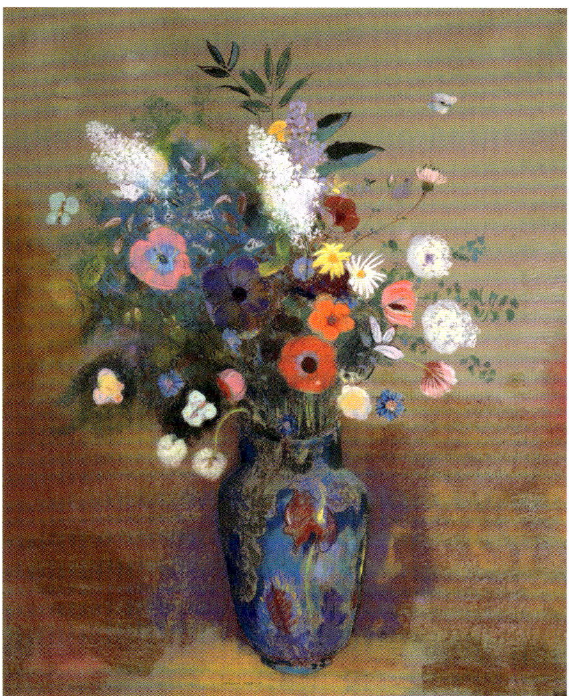

Odilon Redon
Bouquet of Flowers, c. 1900–05
Pastel on paper
31⅝ × 25¼ in. (80.3 × 64.1 cm)
The Metropolitan Museum of Art
Gift of Mrs. George B. Post, 1956

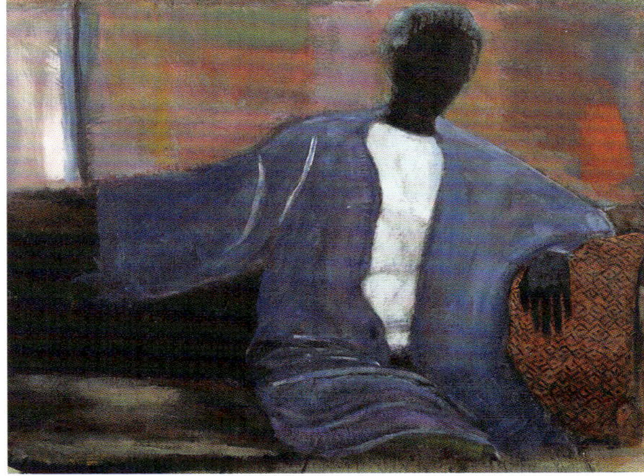

Reggie Burrows Hodges
Seated Listener: Orange Pillow, 2020
Acrylic and pastel on linen
38 × 50 in. (96.5 × 127 cm)

The first time I saw the work of Reggie Burrows Hodges—images from an exhibition preview that crossed my email inbox in January 2021—his paintings made me think of Odilon Redon's pastel drawing *Bouquet of Flowers* (c. 1900–05). As a teenager, I had a poster of the Redon on the door of my bedroom closet, during which time the emotional sensibility of the work became fixed in my memory. The loose quality of Redon's pastel rendering of flowers—blooms floating off the surface of the brown paper support—came to mind when I encountered Hodges's compositions of seated figures and backyard scenes, rich with atmospheric color resting on the surface of the blackest black you can imagine. In that moment of first viewing, Hodges's paintings, and their evocation of Redon, held for me an inherent compellingness I couldn't quite put my finger on.

In both *Bouquet of Flowers* and Hodges's *Seated Listener: Orange Pillow* (2020), hazy fields of color surround the compositions' subjects. These passages are marked by an indistinctness—a crucial vagueness of detail—that is central to this sensibility I'm trying to describe. In the Redon, the vase of flowers is not located in a specific interior; instead, its setting is barely suggested by a scumble of rust brown shifting into warm purple, with touches of apricot and dark pink. Similarly, in *Seated Listener, Orange Pillow*, the figure's head and shoulders are surrounded by abstract modulations of brown-tinged purple, purple-orange, dusty green, smoky periwinkle, and orange-pink. The setting is less a defined place than an environment of color. Not long after my first encounter with Hodges's paintings, I was able to understand something about his works' intrinsic compellingness while watching a Zoom conversation between Hodges and writer Hilton Als, in which the artist made an offhand comment about his mindset when painting: "I don't tend to paint thinking of what the thing should look like . . . I'm *really* concerned about, *how does it feel*."

How does it feel. Hodges's appeal to how a painting *feels* is the golden thread that connects his otherwise wide-ranging subjects. In his paintings, we are presented with scenes whose details may be loosely rendered, but whose emotional precision is sharp as a knife point, ready to pierce. Trying to describe the emotional sharpness of Hodges's paintings, I'm reminded of Roland Barthes's moving writings about the *punctum* of photography—a quality he described as "that accident which pricks me (but also bruises me, is poignant to me)."[1] For Barthes, the punctum was predicated on the "truth" of photography—the "real" of the photographic image; its ability to attest to "*that-has-been*."[2] Hodges's paintings, by contrast, have a piercing emotional quality precisely because they are *not* photographs. In different versions of *Swimming in Compton*, for example, the kidney-shaped backyard pool of Hodges's childhood home changes in its contours, its form subtly morphing from painting to painting. Likewise, the pool's surrounding backyard shifts across different canvases, revealing itself in varying degrees of abstractness and detail. *Swimming in Compton: Red Towel* (2020) shows us the curves of the pool, the hardscape of the pool deck, the edge of a covered patio structure, and an impressionistic sense of the far side of the backyard. *Swimming in Compton: Big Pots* (2020) could be a different place entirely, its background resembling a Rothko painting with semi-rectangular color fields of yellowish sky and blue water hovering over a dark ground. These

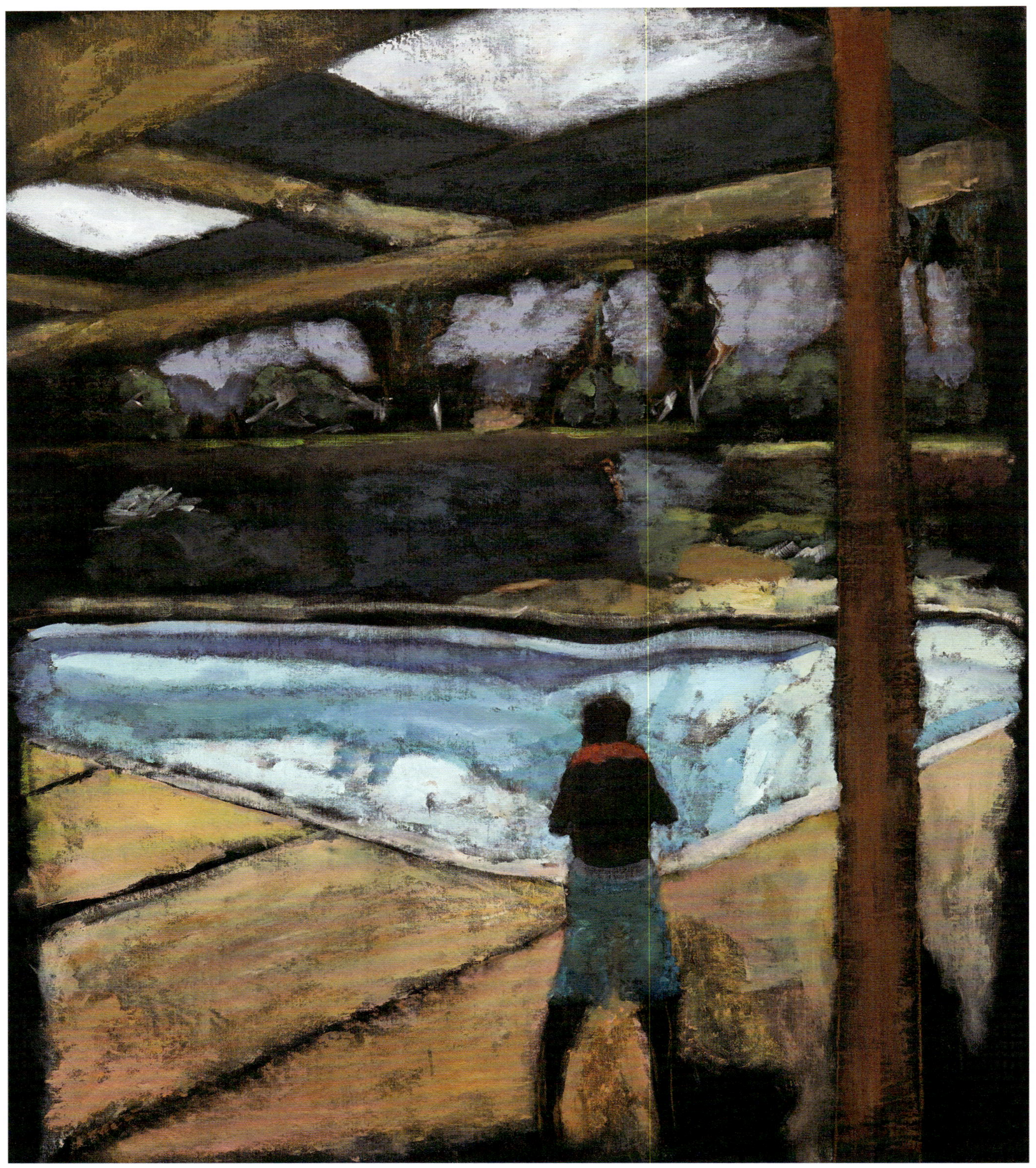

Reggie Burrows Hodges
Swimming in Compton: Red Towel, 2020
Acrylic and pastel on linen
56 × 48 in. (142 × 122 cm)

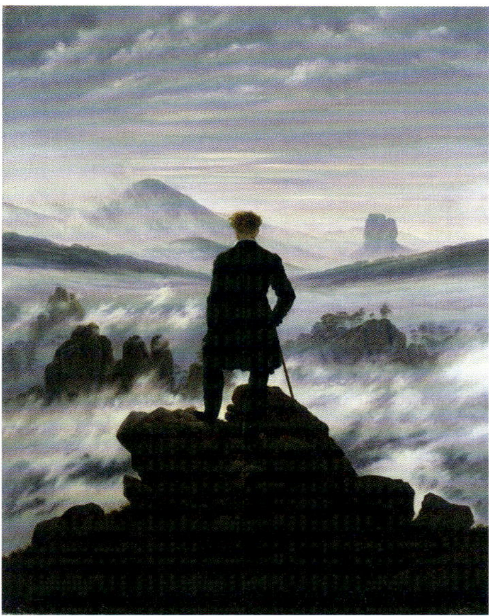

Caspar David Friedrich
Wanderer above the Sea of Fog, c. 1817
Oil on canvas
47 × 39⅛ in. (119.5 × 99.5 cm)
Hamburger Kunsthalle

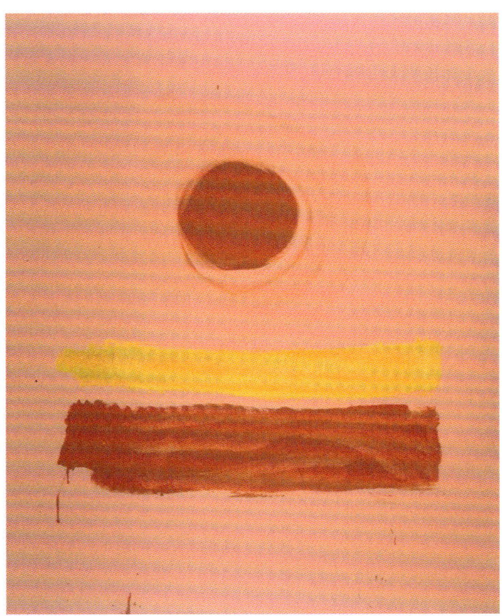

Adolph Gottlieb
Russet, 1973
Acrylic on canvas
60 × 48 in. (152.4 × 121.9 cm)

examples are intimately connected, though, by the lone, towel-wearing figure in each composition, back to the viewer, who gazes out onto the scene. Like the German Romantic *Rückenfigur* made famous by Caspar David Friedrich, Hodges's subject gives us both a visual and emotional vantage point we can imagine stepping into—a place from which to access how the paintings *feel*. Here, Hodges gives us not the photographic facticity of what these scenes looked like, but the poignancy of memory's abstract, impressionistic visual record, where feeling overwhelms fact.

This distinction between knowledge and feeling is how I first structured my understanding of Hodges's abstract works, too—namely, the three large-scale paintings based on the tennis line-calling technology Hawk-Eye, which also gives the exhibition its name. These works initially surprised me, given how different they are from Hodges's figurative paintings. As a non-tennis player, I had no visual associations to call on when first reading about the works' origins. Unlike the intuitive response I experience when encountering Hodges's figurative paintings (that unnamable compellingness), I felt challenged with his abstractions to understand how these unexpected canvases relate to the question of feeling that infuses his other works.

When I first viewed *Hawk-Eye: Pink and Green* (2019), *Fault* (2021), and *Wide* (2021), I knew they related to a line-calling system, but I thought the black oval shapes represented the shadow of a ball passing over the painted lines of a tennis court. Even after reading that Hawk-Eye uses a system of computer-linked cameras, I imagined the technology to be akin to the instant replay system in major league baseball, where we get to see a recorded playback of what actually happened in slowed-down time. Eventually, YouTube videos about how the Hawk-Eye system works, and broadcast clips from prominent tennis matches utilizing the technology, enlightened me about the visual references for Hodges's elongated ovals, and their relationship to knowledge and vision. As I learned, Hawk-Eye uses cameras positioned around a court to calculate a ball's trajectory and mathematically model where it will land. The system then illustrates the arc of the ball and its predicted landing point through a computer-generated image. Amidst the lines and curves of Hawk-Eye's calculations, the elongated oval represents the computer-calculated surface area of contact between the ball and the court.

So how do Hodges's Hawk-Eye paintings *feel*? I realize it's not an intuitive question to ask. Putting aside the disconcerting sci-fi aspect of Hawk-Eye's predictive assurances (it's "never wrong"), the geometric vocabulary Hodges appropriates for these compositions would seem to lie squarely on the *knowledge* end of the knowledge-feeling spectrum. Rather than attesting "*that-has-been*," Hawk-Eye's computer imagery argues "*that-will-be*." Moreover, were it not for the tennis references in their titles, Hodges's paintings could be viewed as pure abstractions—as likely to be in dialogue with abstract works by Adolph Gottlieb as with Hodges's own figurative paintings that reference his experience as an elite tennis player. In *Fault*, there's a lush, velvet painterliness to Hodges's application of pink over green; a satisfying asymmetry to the composition that's energized by the diagonal axis of the black oval in the lower-left quadrant.

To help me think through Hodges's Hawk-Eye paintings, I want to detour for a moment to the Referees series in *Hawkeye*. Though referencing scenes from sports other than tennis (the indistinct settings of these paintings appear to be soccer or football fields, punctuated by the abstract dapple of spectators in stands), Hodges's Referees, in their emotional tenor, recall his seminal body of tennis-themed paintings bearing titles such as *In the Service of Others* and *For the Greater Good*—quietly piercing works in which he shines a light on the community of supporting figures (individuals holding umbrellas over players to shade them from the sun; ball kids waiting patiently courtside, hands behind their backs) who give of their time, care, and attention to enable the athletic achievements of a selected few. This principle of recognition is present in the Referees paintings, as well as in other works featuring sports officials—for example, *Single Source* (2019) and *Surveillance* (2019)—in which Hodges presents us with the unassuming labor of individuals engaged in acts of conferring, making calls, and watching game play.

What I haven't addressed until this point is the centrality of blackness in Hodges's practice. The construction of his paintings begins with his matte black grounds, a physical starting point and conceptual foundation Hodges masterfully conceives of as "blackness in totality." From these grounds, his subjects, whether athletes, family members, or solitary figures, gradually materialize to form a community of blackness—a painted world where his subjects are depicted in straightforward acts of being, seeing, and being seen. To anyone who has viewed his paintings in person, Hodges's emotional investment in his figurative subjects is evident at every stroke.

During the course of my self-education about Hawk-Eye technology, I learned about a 2004 US Open quarterfinal between Serena Williams and Jennifer Capriati that became infamous for the number of bad calls—clearly visible to at-home television spectators—that were unfairly levied against Williams in favor of Capriati by an umpire named Mariana Alves. Taking place when Hawk-Eye was already in use by television networks, but not by match officials, the egregiousness of the bias on display was sufficient to make most viewers experience an excess of feeling—a fact I readily discovered through my own outrage when watching clips of these calls and Hawk-Eye's findings to the contrary. In *Citizen: An American Lyric*, poet Claudia Rankine cuts to the essence of the match when she reflects, in her incisive prose, "Though no one was saying anything explicitly about Serena's black body, you are not the only viewer who thought it was getting in the way of Alves's sight line."[3]

It's tempting, at first, to associate Hodges's Hawk-Eye paintings with the infamous 2004 match. Viewed in this context, they certainly occupy the expanse between knowledge and feeling—pitting the certainty of the elongated ovals against those infuriating failures of sight and the broader injustices they represent. But knowing Hodges and his generosity of spirit, I suspect there's a different way to understand these compositions that speaks more to empathy than antagonism. A clue comes in the subtitle of *Referees: Ally* (2021). Here, Hodges's choice of the word *ally* tells me that within the community of blackness he crafts

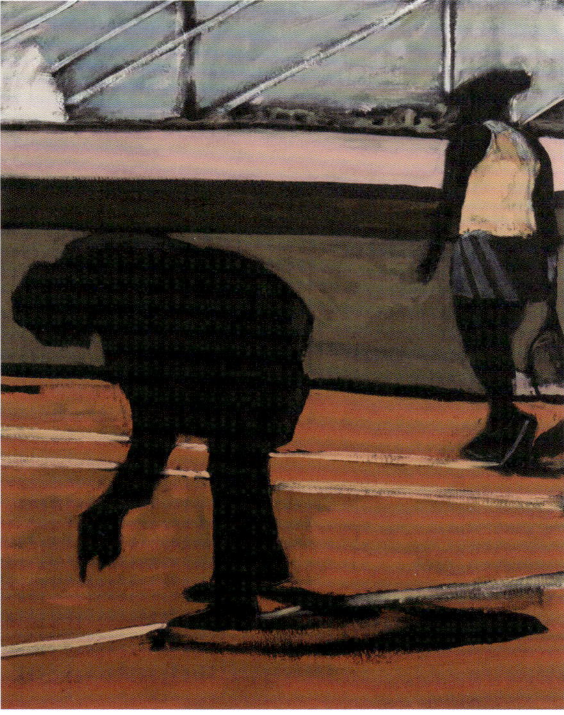

Reggie Burrows Hodges
Single Source, 2019
Acrylic and pastel on canvas
60 × 46¼ in. (152.4 × 117.5 cm)

into being, the referees, line umpires, and other sports officials he depicts are not adversaries rendering unfair calls, but individuals whose painted presence is offered to us in metaphoric service of our basic human desire to believe someone is looking out for us, ready to intercede against the fouls that come our way.

The last works I want to discuss are the portraits of Hodges's parents that anchor the exhibition. The most beautiful example is the full-length portrait of his mother, *Melba 77* (2021). With its incredible paint handling, deep color palette, and brilliant contrast between the figure's densely patterned dress and her broadly painted surroundings, this work bruises me, to borrow Barthes's phrase. I could look at it for hours and still not be able to spell out what makes it so compelling. But it's Hodges's *Father's Self-Portrait* (2019) that finally unlocks for me the question of *feeling* in his Hawk-Eye paintings. In contrast to the indistinctness of so many of his painted settings, the backdrop of *Father's Self-Portrait* is unusually well-defined. Whether coincidental or not, the olive-green wall and floor that fill the background of the portrait, and the deep-pink and grayish-white architectural accents that structure the shallow space, suggest for me the green, pink, and white tones of Hodges's abstract Hawk-Eye canvases. I know this connection may be a stretch of my own visual making, but with this affinity in mind, Hodges's abstract paintings feel to me like statements of bittersweet longing—an ache for the watchful gaze of family members, referees, and other allies. The Hawk-Eye system's computer-brain may be a proxy for the human eye of a beholder, but a machine can never know us; its computer-drawn image may be infallibly accurate, but it doesn't enable us to feel *seen*.

At the outset of this essay, I suggested that the space between knowledge and feeling is how I first attempted to understand Hodges's Hawk-Eye paintings. I want to end by amending that understanding. In puzzling through my relationship to this body of work, at the back of my mind was always the idea, planted by the artist's own reflections, that how a painting *feels* has the capacity to override knowledge. In my rudimentary understanding of Hodges's comment, I mentally placed emotion and fact at two opposite ends of a spectrum. What I realize now, after weaving through the connective threads that tie together the works in *Hawkeye*, is an essential lesson of Hodges's paintings: knowledge, it turns out, *is* a question of feeling.

1   Roland Barthes, *Camera Lucida: Reflections on Photography* (New York: Farrar, Straus, and Giroux, 1981), 27.

2   Ibid., 77.

3   Claudia Rankine, *Citizen: An American Lyric* (Minneapolis, MN: Graywolf Press, 2014), 27.

Anjulie Rao
Fault Lines

As children, my sister and I would create our own games. Not like the riffs on hide-and-seek or tag, whose innumerable iterations were exercised in gym class or at summer camp—our games were, we believed, wholly unique to the genre of sports. Some borrowed equipment from activities like soccer or badminton, but most required handcrafted tools that we would use to swat at balls of duct tape or Barbie heads. We built vehicles from flimsy plastic storage bins with wheels and raced down hills, armed with a claw made of spoons haphazardly taped together, attempting to chase a soccer ball.

Much of the time spent inventing games was occupied by complex negotiations of rules and procedures. Each game required a series of hypothetical considerations: what if the ball rolls into the gutter; what if the driver tips their cart; what if your spoon-claw comes undone? As an adult I now believe that the pleasure of inventing games wasn't limited to play, but rather, in the creation of rules and guidelines that kept the competition fair and ourselves accountable to each other. For a few hours in our short lives, we were the queens of our world. We could exempt ourselves from bedtime by mandating that the game be played at night or excuse ourselves from dinner early because we were in the quarterfinals. Our parents were, understandably, flummoxed—who, really, was in charge during game time?

When confronted with the enormous task of penning words around Reggie Burrows Hodges's new body of work, I was struck by his depictions of both rule-makers and the rules themselves. Human figures, when present, are defined by their environments, and identity is subject to external forces—ah, what a metaphor for childhood's regulations, those values of truth and fairness that govern our young selves and continue to guide us into adulthood. But those rules are set by adults whose identities have been shaped by previous lines drawn between fairness and unfairness, truth and fiction—they are in some ways arbitrary. But what does that then say about identity?

Fault

Later on, when I began teaching writing at the School of the Art Institute of Chicago, I learned that my students were experiencing a rift between their childhood—who they "were"—and adulthood, defined not by who they had become, but rather, the void ahead of them. Each semester since 2018, students have penned essays about their parents' grandeur. They are often described as imposing, fastidious adults, at times distant from their families because of their focus on work. Examining Salvador Dali's *A Chemist Lifting with Extreme Precaution the Cuticle of a Grand Piano* (1936), one student wrote that the man faintly visible in the background holding the edge of a piano transformed into her father; the young, faceless boy looking on represented herself:

> In particular, the image of the man stepping on paper reminded me of my father, who was immersed in his work and didn't care about others. In the past, my father was very stressed at work and spent very little time at home," she wrote. "I always waited for him; I missed his

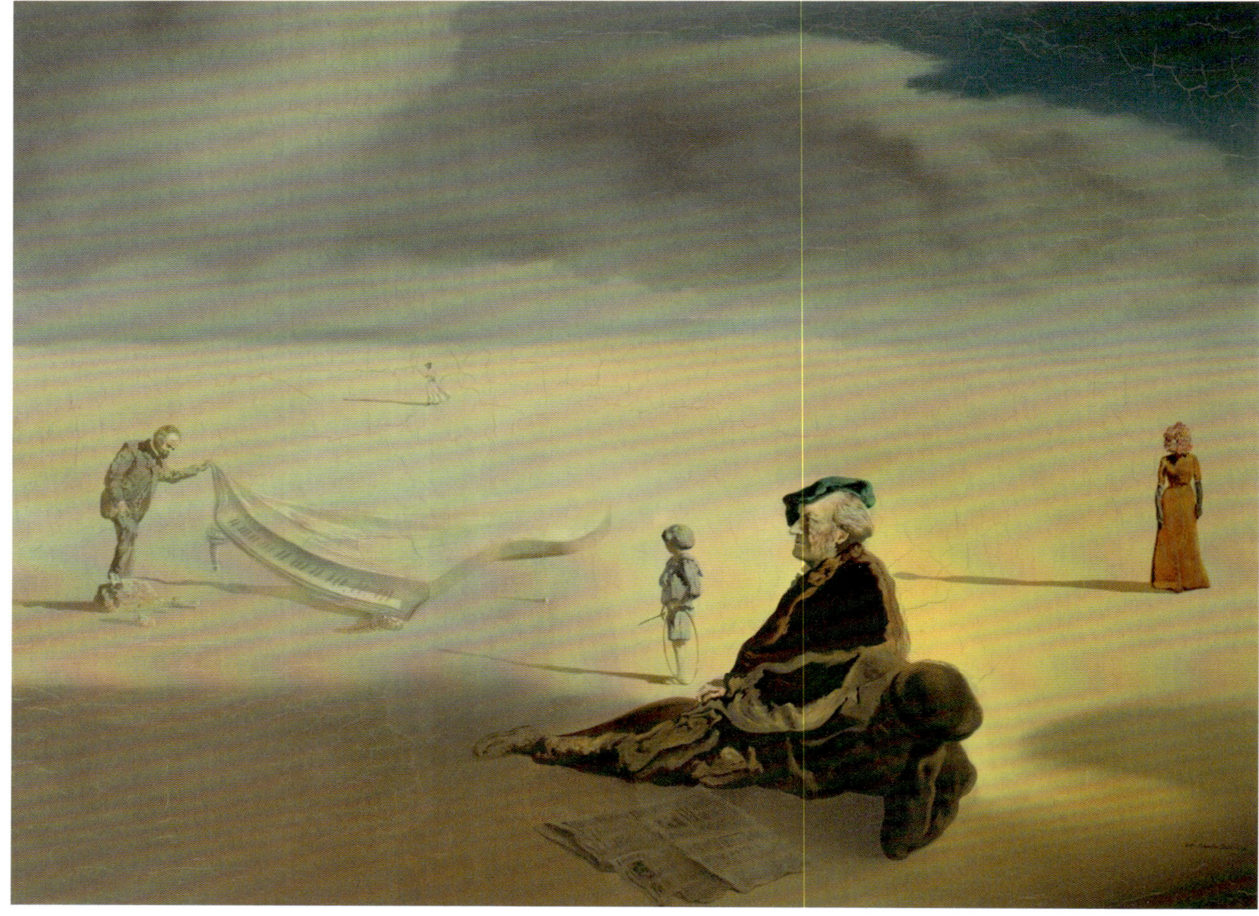

Salvador Dalí
A Chemist Lifting with Extreme Precaution the Cuticle of a Grand Piano, 1936
Oil on canvas
19 × 25¼ in. (48.3 × 64.1 cm)
Art Institute of Chicago; Gift of Mr. and Mrs. Joseph R. Shapiro

existence. Now that I think about it . . . I know how he feels about sac-
rificing for his family, but I couldn't think of this when I was young.

About this sacrifice, she went on to say, her father felt regret; she learned as
an adult that his dedication to his job was, indeed, his devotion to her. Though
his work took time away from his family, she had grown to understand that his
labor crossed an invisible boundary between what the love of a parent feels
like—care, presence, togetherness—and how love manifests as sacrifice. It
revealed a new truth about the power of work itself, one that could no longer
be defined by the boundaries set by the authorities in her young world. She could
no longer judge him for these actions and decisions. Like myself and the myriad
other young writers who have expounded upon our parents as subject, she came to
find that the people who raised her are, simply, people. They make choices, they
craft rules, they set boundaries; all of those creations are as fallible as the design-
ers themselves. These boundaries are significant—if not predominant—because
they are defined by the fault line.

Melba 77

From what I've gleaned from Lacan—or more specifically, those who have
attempted to teach me Lacan—this experience of discovering one's parents is
akin to the mirror phase, in which a child recognizes that their own reflection in
a mirror is distinct from that of their parents. The sensation of "I am of that, but I
am not that" becomes predominant in the formation of identity. The mirror phase
then characterizes desire; a desire to return to the moment in which a person discovered themselves as separate, severed from their previous form. That desire, or
objet petit a, becomes a burning need to locate oneself in the other.

I think often of Alfred Hitchcock's MacGuffin, a fictional narrative device used
to drive plot forward. The MacGuffin has a heavy presence in the storyline; perhaps it is a monster terrorizing a city or an ominous event for which characters
are rigorously preparing. Its centrality is what motivates each character to act or
respond, yet the MacGuffin itself is insignificant to the story. Instead, what mat-
ters is the effect of that object. Writing in *The Sublime Object of Ideology*, Slavoj
Žižek compares Lacan's *objet petit a* to the MacGuffin, which he describes as
"the lack, the remainder of the Real that sets in motion the symbolic movement
of interpretation, a hole at the center of the symbolic order, the mere appearance of
some secret to be explained, interpreted."[1] The discovery of ourselves happens
only when our own MacGuffins—the rules of truth, the values that charge our
understanding of right and wrong— are unearthed.

Looking at Hodges's *Melba 77* (2021), I am struck by this portrait of adulthood.
A woman dressed in a vibrant robe stands over a percolator. Her profile is shaped
by the shelving and walls behind her. Though she possesses no distinguishable
facial features, her posture—right hip leaning against the counter, head cocked
downward toward her task—is familiar; an adult savoring one rare, quiet moment
in the beginning of the day. I compare it instinctively to *Father's Self - Portrait*

(2017–19), in which a man, sporting a robe and gripping the newspaper, is also immersed in a morning routine. Yet unlike the woman in *Melba 77*, his face is rendered by light; his nose and cheekbones are framed by a brown hue and the crest of his lip seems to cast a shadow. It is, perhaps, 10 am on a Sunday. I am beginning to believe that this is not the father's self-portrait but rather a self-portrait of the artist as he begins to see himself defined by his father's presence.

Perhaps this work, like my students' reflections, represents a second mirror phase, in which we don't see ourselves as separate entities from our parents, but instead focus on the precise ways in which they shaped us. Certainly, our lifetime of humiliations and traumas and moments of joy might contribute to a sense of confidence or purpose, but in distinguishing our understanding of truth and fairness from those who have historically defined them for us, we begin to see ourselves more clearly.

Referees: And Then There Were Three

Nothing grows in isolation, as I learned from Roland Barthes's meditations on solitude. In "Suspending Events, Loving the Margin: Solitude According to Barthes," Sabine Hillen discusses the crushing pressures of "smooth time" versus "idiorhythmic time," or the ability to manage one's own time apart from or within a community. The notion of "smooth time" describes how a society that imposes rules of engagement drives individuals out of that community—creating hermits. Yet it is impossible to live in total solitude; the only way to build community is to develop one's own rhythm of participating in and moving away from a society, creating what Hillen calls a "socialism of distances."[2] In some ways, it seems we must move in and out of our determined, imposed roles in order to live together.

In playing games of our own design, we become our own referees, blowing whistles on ourselves in moments that, we can only hope, we recognize as our own self-violations. Once the rules are set, they cannot be changed by the players; only those who wear the whistle can decide what constitutes unfairness or flagrant infractions. When it was just the two of us, we had to take turns being the referee. Sometimes I would don the proverbial black-and-white stripes; other times it was my sister calling foul. We move between these roles to build a collective experience of fairness.

We experience the fallibility of our parents not only by seeing ourselves as products of their rules, but also through the failing of our parents' bodies, and at times, their minds. Those people who once defined us through values instilled and regulations enforced will become dust; what will become of us—our selves, our understanding of who we are as individuals—when they are gone?

This is not a unique question to ask oneself when facing the loss of a rule-maker. But I turn to Robert Nozick's *The Examined Life* in an effort to rebuild my confidence for the time in which truth and fairness will become mine to define:

Being a parent helps one become a better child, a more forgiving grown-up child of one's parents, whom one now must act the parent to. . . . When children are young, it is the task of parents to manage the relationship, to monitor it and keep it continuing on a somewhat even keel. During some brief period, perhaps, that responsibility becomes more equal, and then, before one has had time to notice it, it becomes the now-grown-up child's task to maintain the relationship, sometimes to pamper parents, to humor them, to avoid subjects that upset them, and to comfort the surviving one. If adolescence is sometimes marked by rebelling against one's parents and adulthood by becoming independent of them, what marks maturity is becoming a parent to them.[3]

The role-reversal from player to referee is a dance we perform while negotiating a grossly unfair reality: that soon we will be on our own. But Nozick's claim that this is a marker of maturity is, I believe, a flawed one. We don't become more mature; rather, we simply switch our costumes, destined to one day return to being an agent of play. The rules that shape us never disappear; rather, they become unavoidable truths that govern our actions and relationships with others. In Hodges's *Tumbler* (2021), an acrobat, mid-backflip, approaches a thick, visually-dominant partition line painted in gray. The painting exudes anxiety, stemming from the tension between the tumbler and the boundary. Will she cross it, perhaps defying that boundary; or will she stick the landing just on the edge? She will decide for herself—there are no others present. She becomes both the referee and the player; we know not where her feet will land.

In this recognition of ourselves not as the sole delineators of truth nor fairness, but instead the products of those definitions as set by the authority of others, we are more clearly able to see ourselves both as individuals and as part of a larger community. We are empowered to decide for ourselves which rules to keep and which to discard. To idiorhythmically occupy those identities—to move from rule-maker to player—we are more clearly able to acknowledge one another and live together. The interplay of ourselves amongst the rules that we've created and the rules to which we've been subjected is vastly complicated, shaping us individually and communally. Though, I'll admit, it never was a simple exercise of building the game.

1   Slavoj Žižek, *The Sublime Object of Ideology* (London: Verso, 1989), 185.

2   Sabine Hillen, "Suspending Events, Loving the Margin: Solitude According to Barthes," trans. Gila Walker, in *Paragraph* 31, no. 1 (2008): 64.

3   Robert Nozick, *Examined Life: Philosophical Meditations* (New York: Simon & Schuster, 1989), 29.

Father's Self-Portrait, 2017–19
Acrylic and pastel on canvas
80 × 68 in. (203.2 × 172.7 cm)

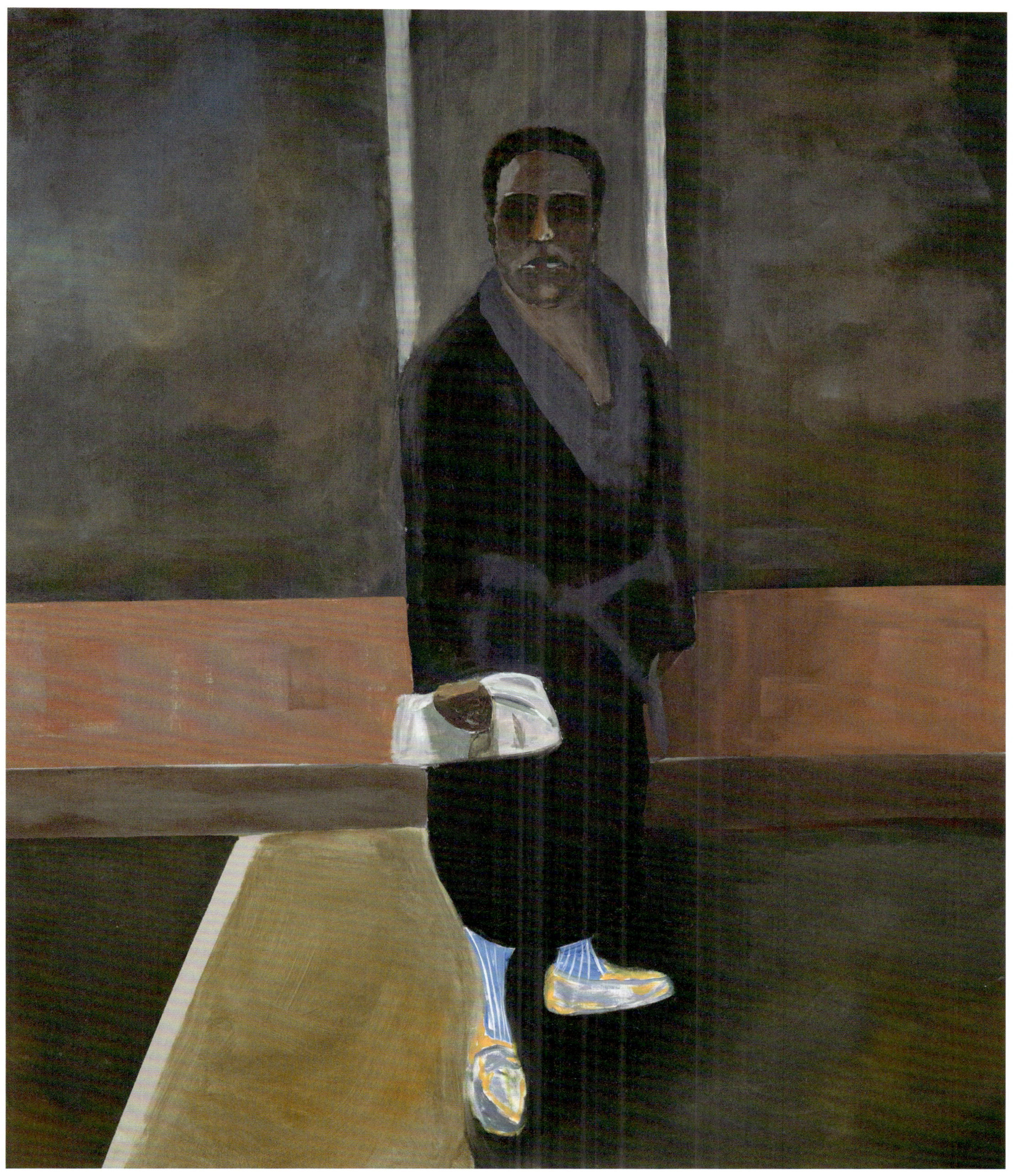

Melba 77, 2021
Acrylic and pastel on linen
70⅛ × 60 in. (178.1 × 152.4 cm)

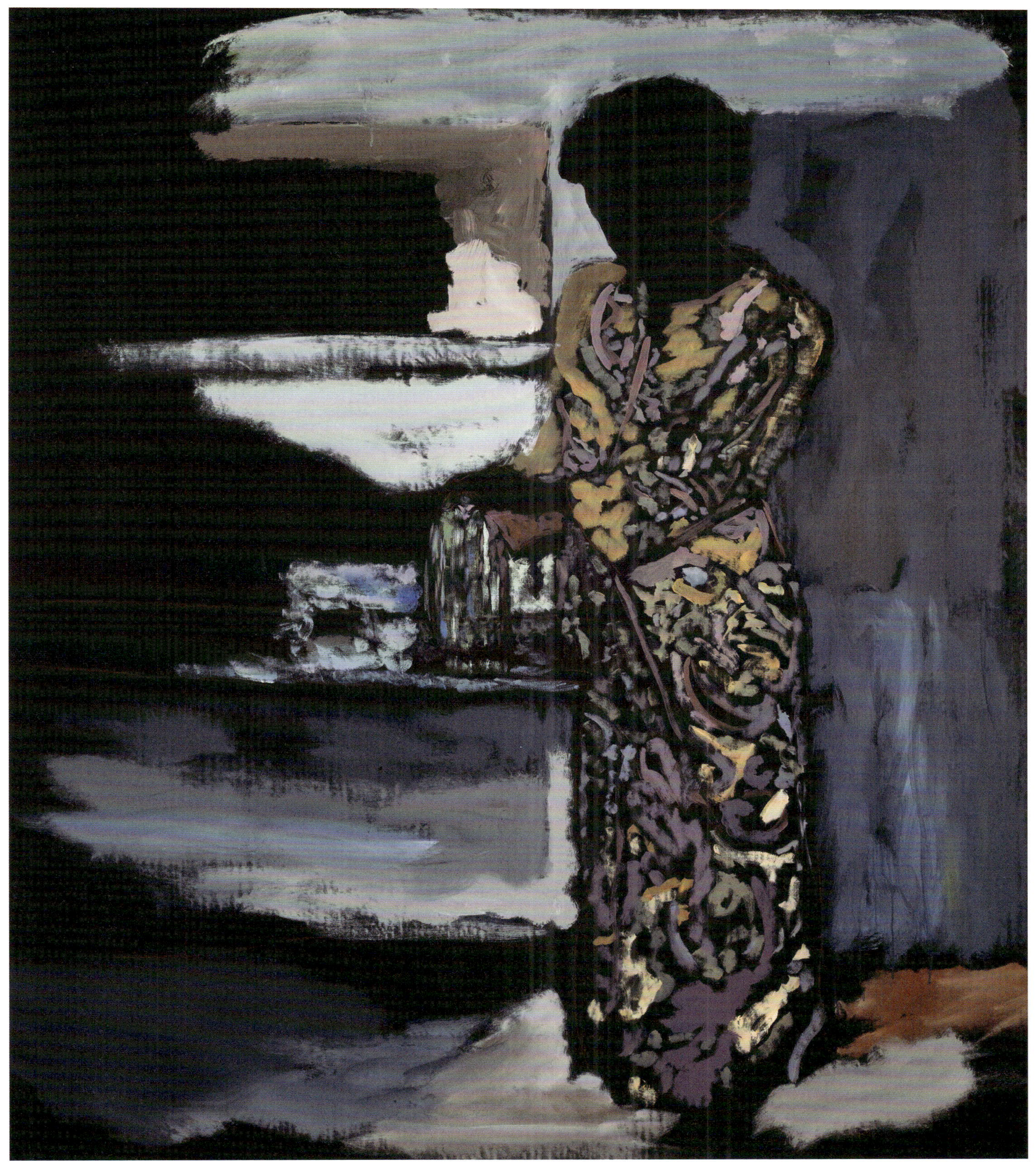

Tumbler, 2021
Acrylic and pastel on linen
71¼ × 83¼ in. (181 × 211.5 cm)

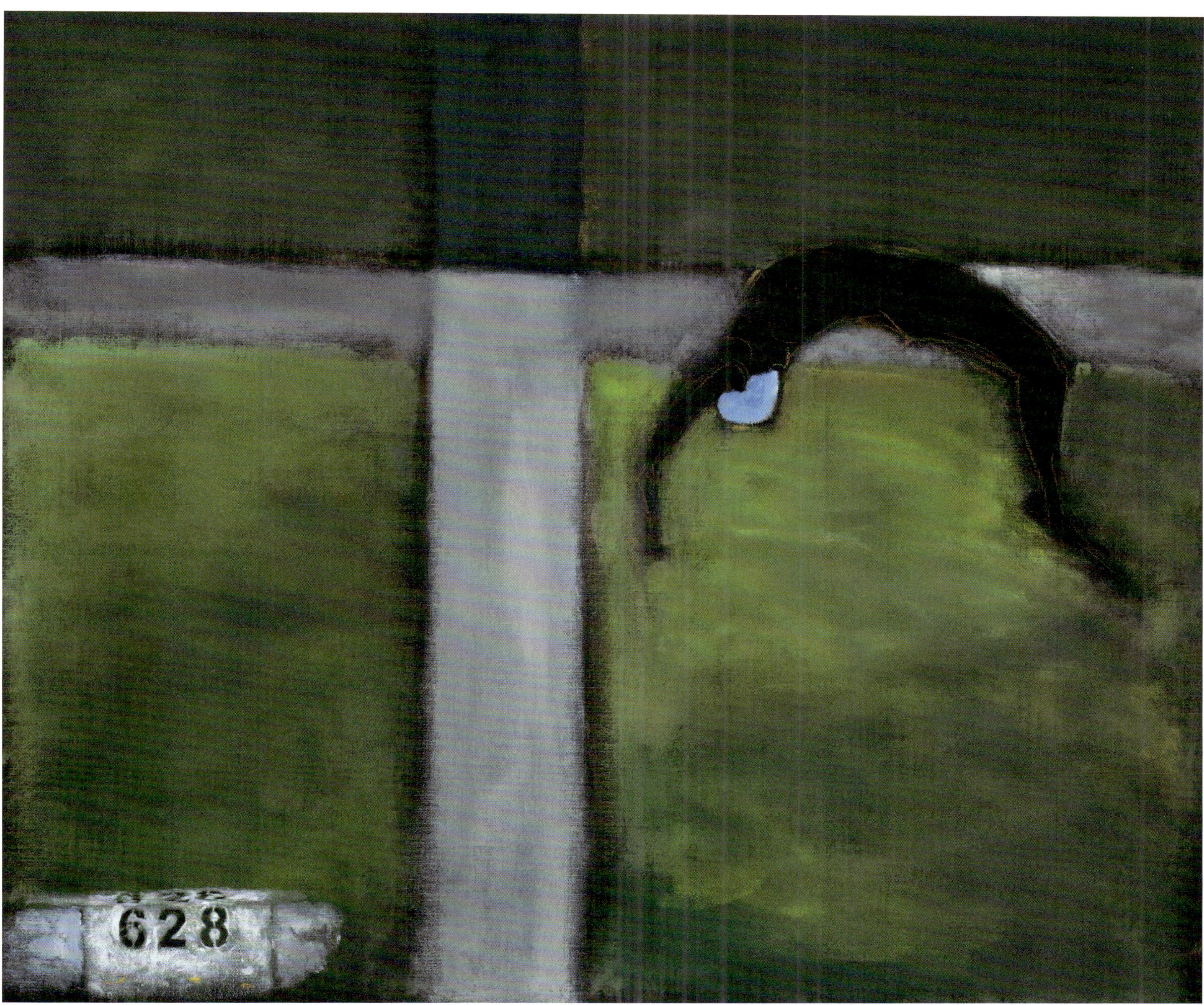
628

Referee: It Stands, 2020
Acrylic and pastel on linen
78 × 68 in. (198.1 × 172.7 cm)

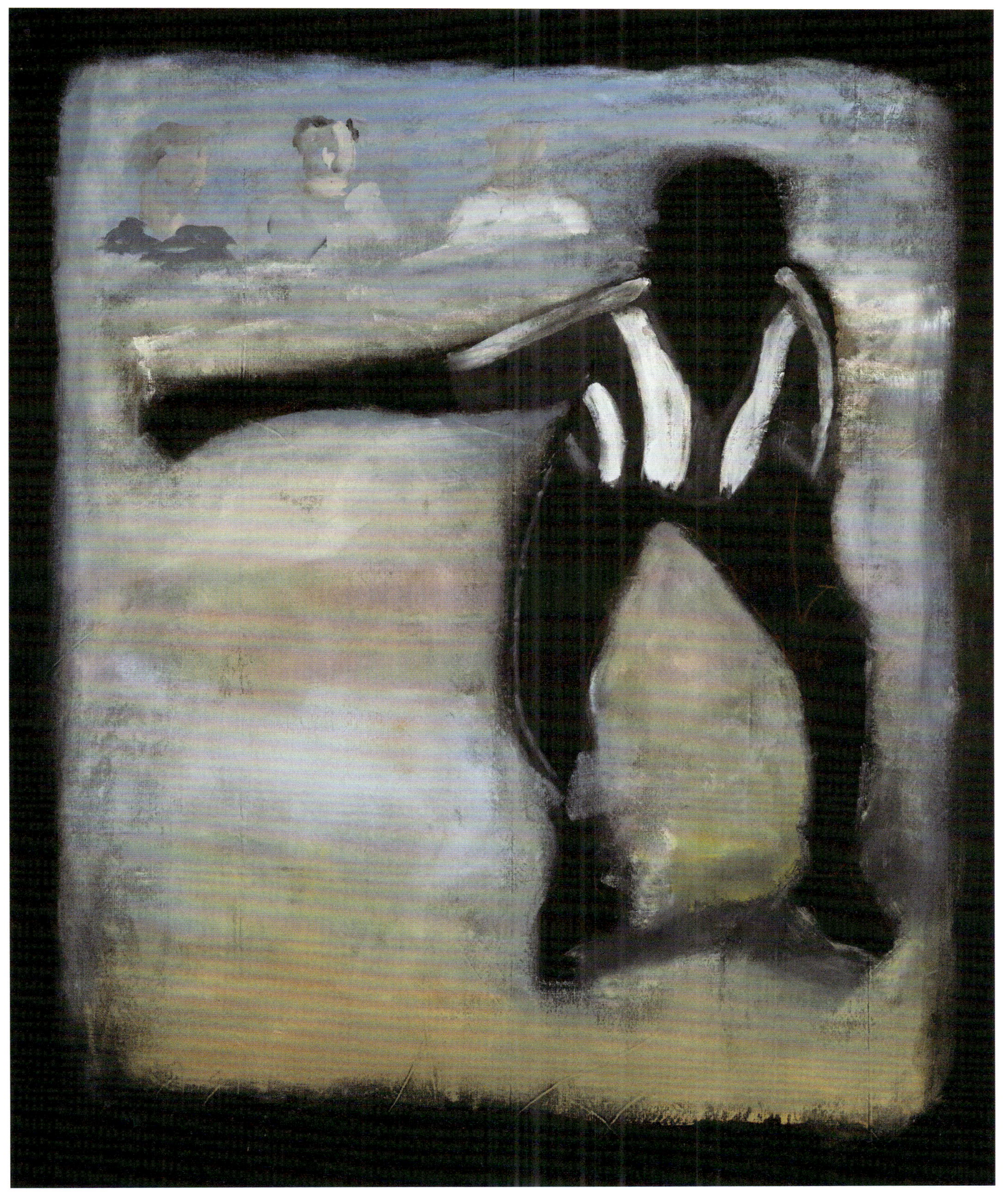

The Story of Alfred: Magenta, 2022
Acrylic and pastel on linen
88 × 97¼ in. (223.5 × 247 cm)

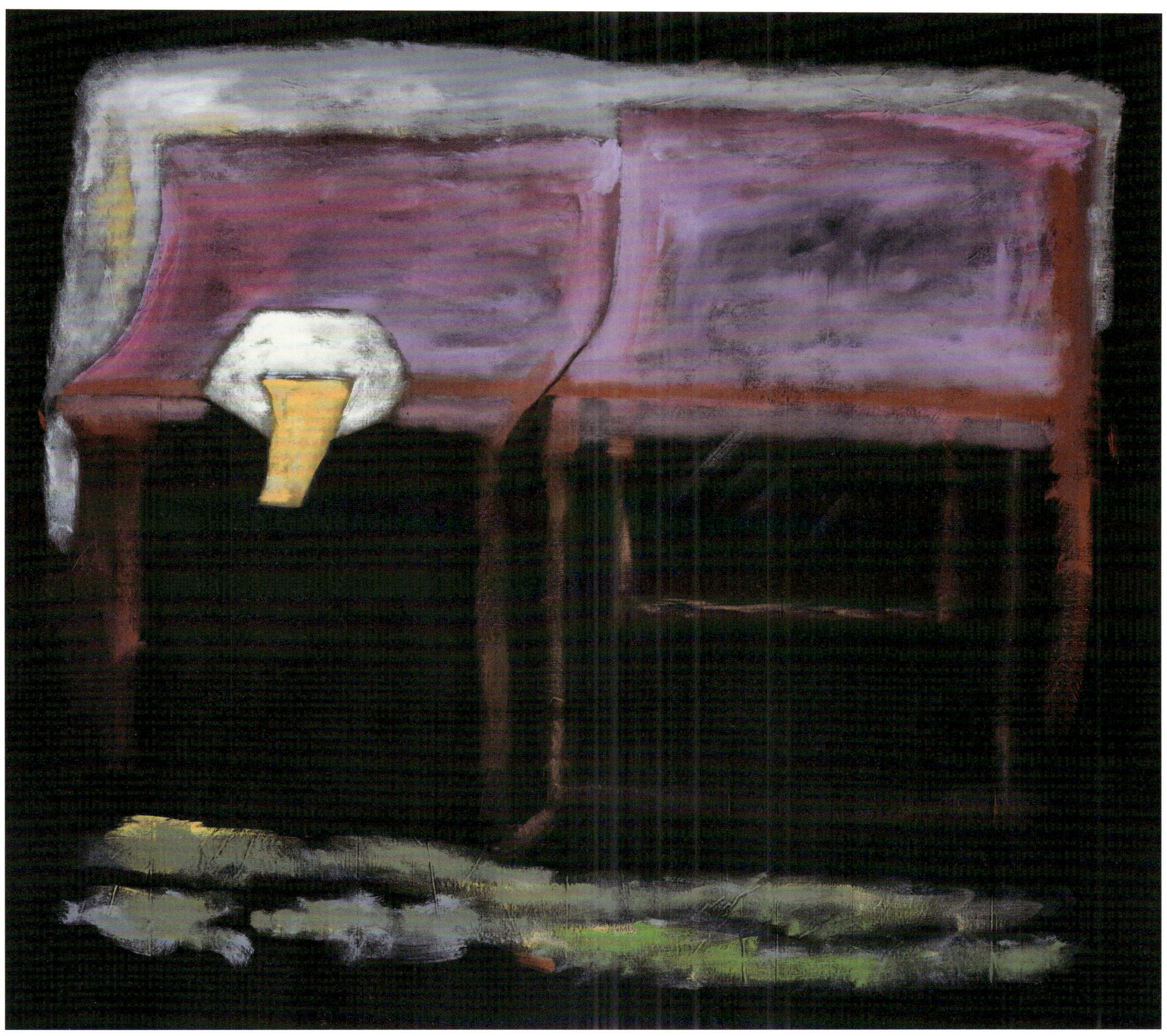

Hawk-Eye: Pink and Green, 2019
Acrylic and pastel on canvas
70¼ × 80¼ in. (178.4 × 203.8 cm)

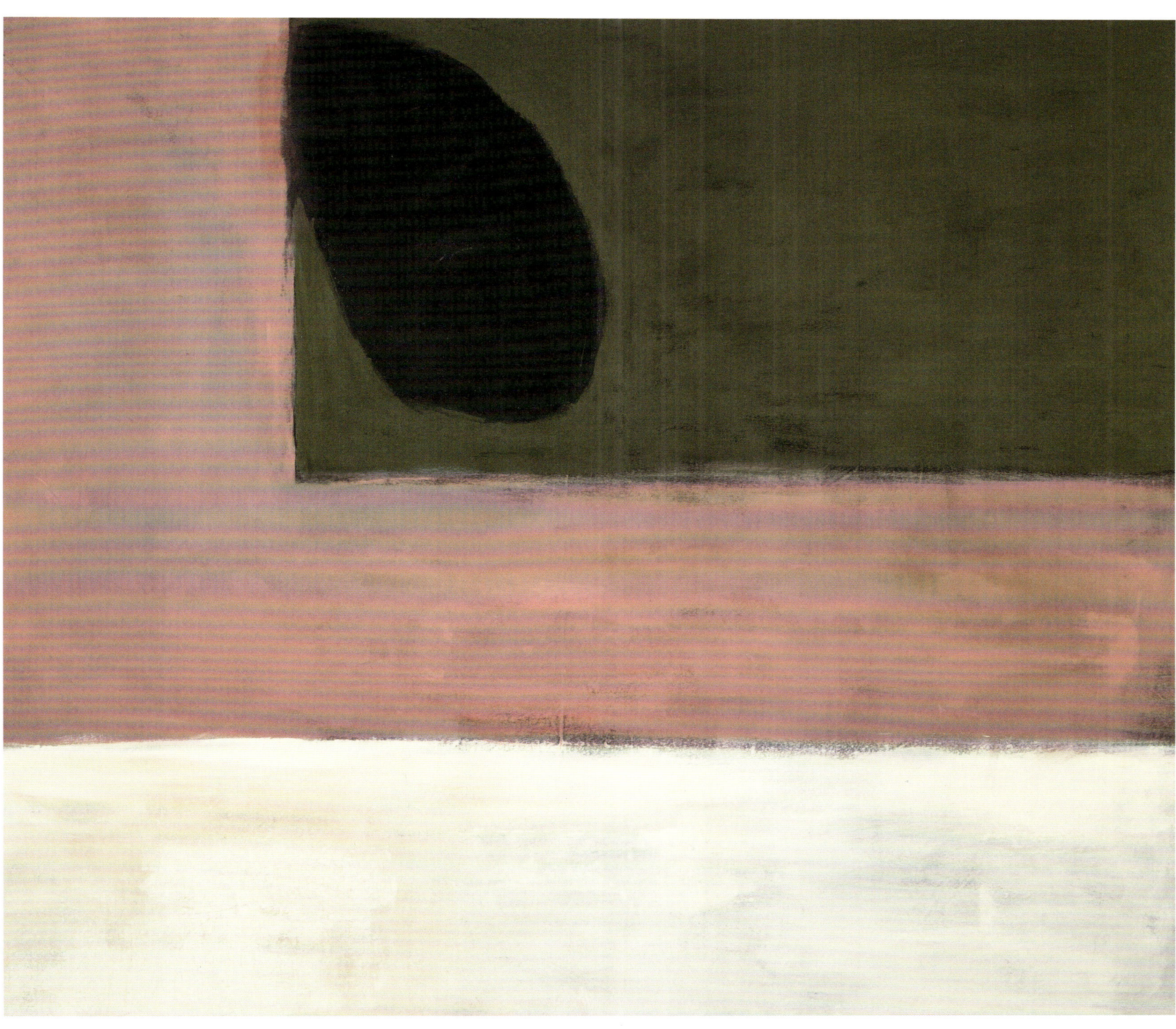

Swimming in Compton: Big Pots, 2020
Acrylic and pastel on linen
79¼ × 66½ in. (201.3 × 168.9 cm)

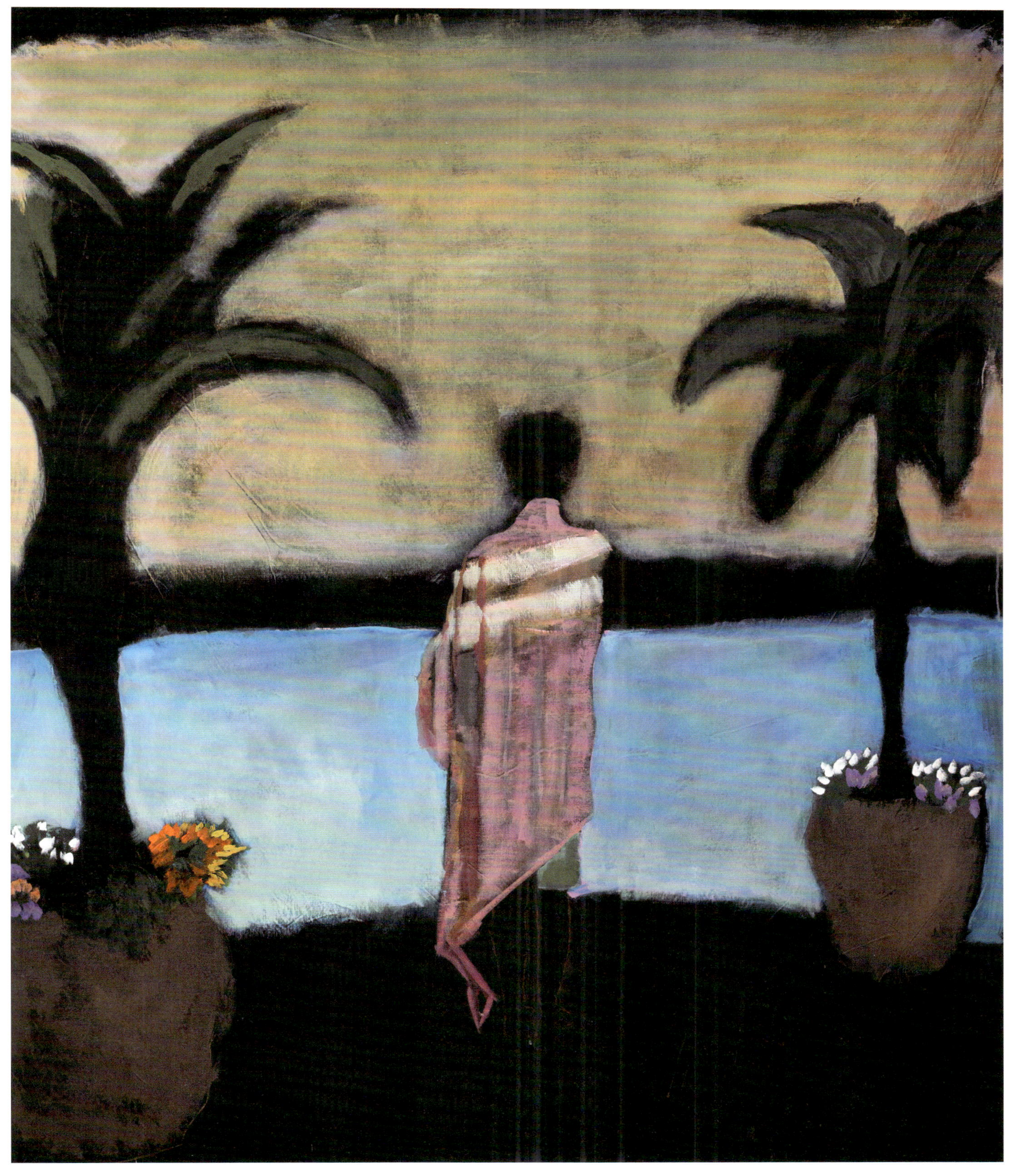

Referees: And Then There Were Three, 2020
Acrylic and pastel on linen
96 × 78 in. (243.8 × 198.1 cm)

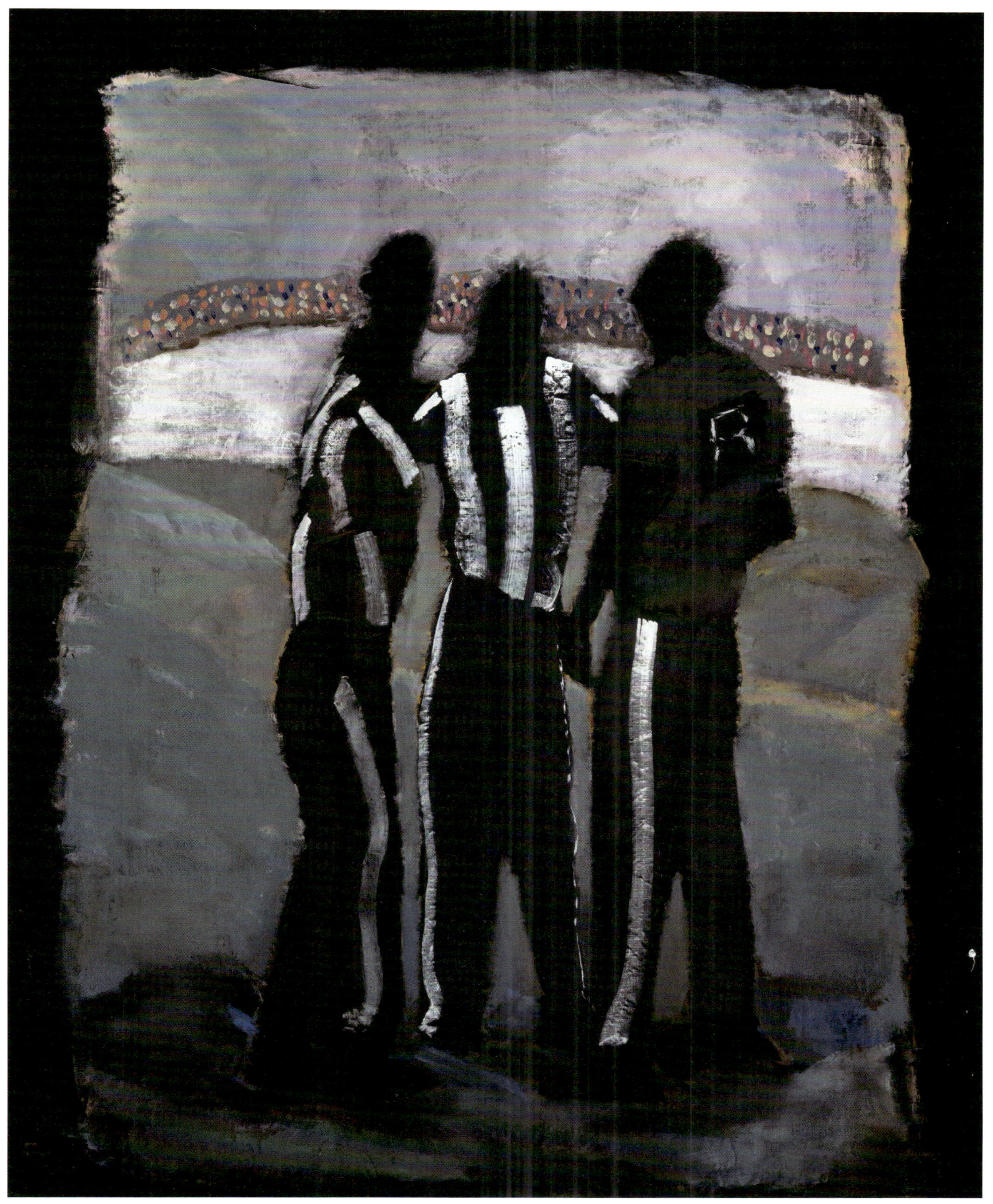

Fault, 2021
Acrylic and pastel on linen
63⅛ × 71⅛ in. (160.4 × 180.7 cm)

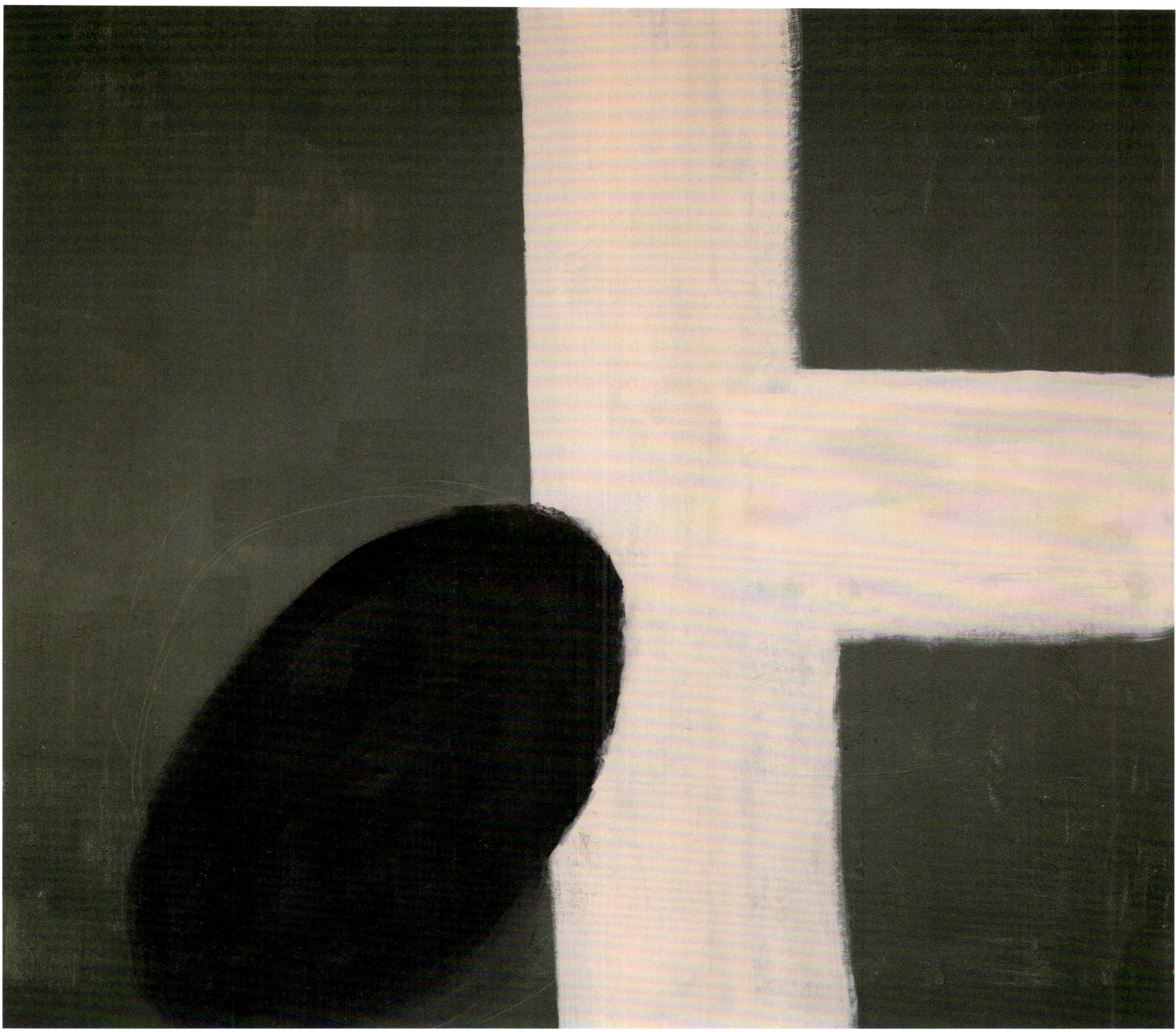

The Story of Ruth, 2021
Acrylic and pastel on linen
83½ × 72½ in. (212.1 × 184.2 cm)

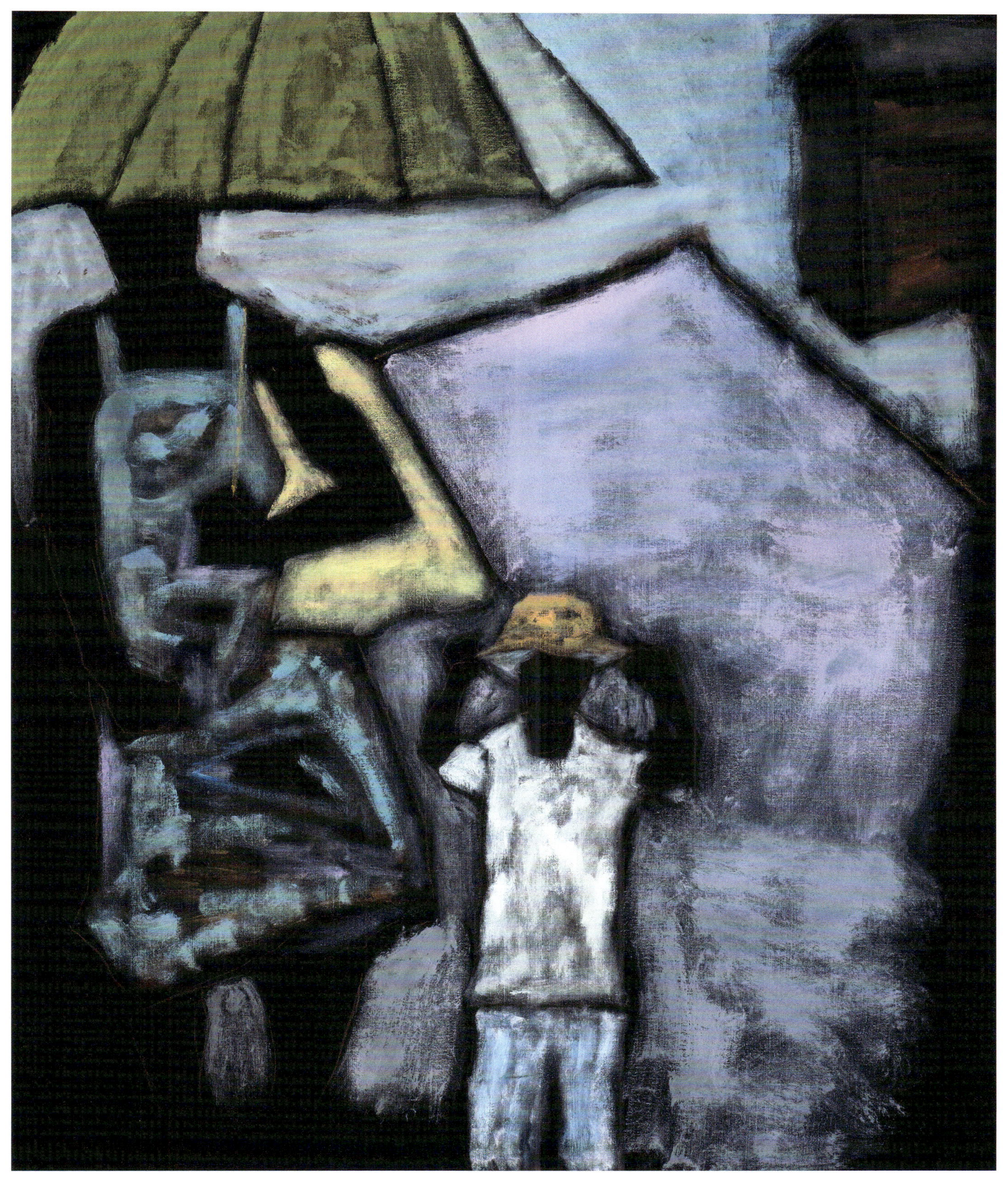

Cannonball: NFJ, 2020
Acrylic and pastel on linen
82½ × 65½ in. (209.6 × 166.4 cm)

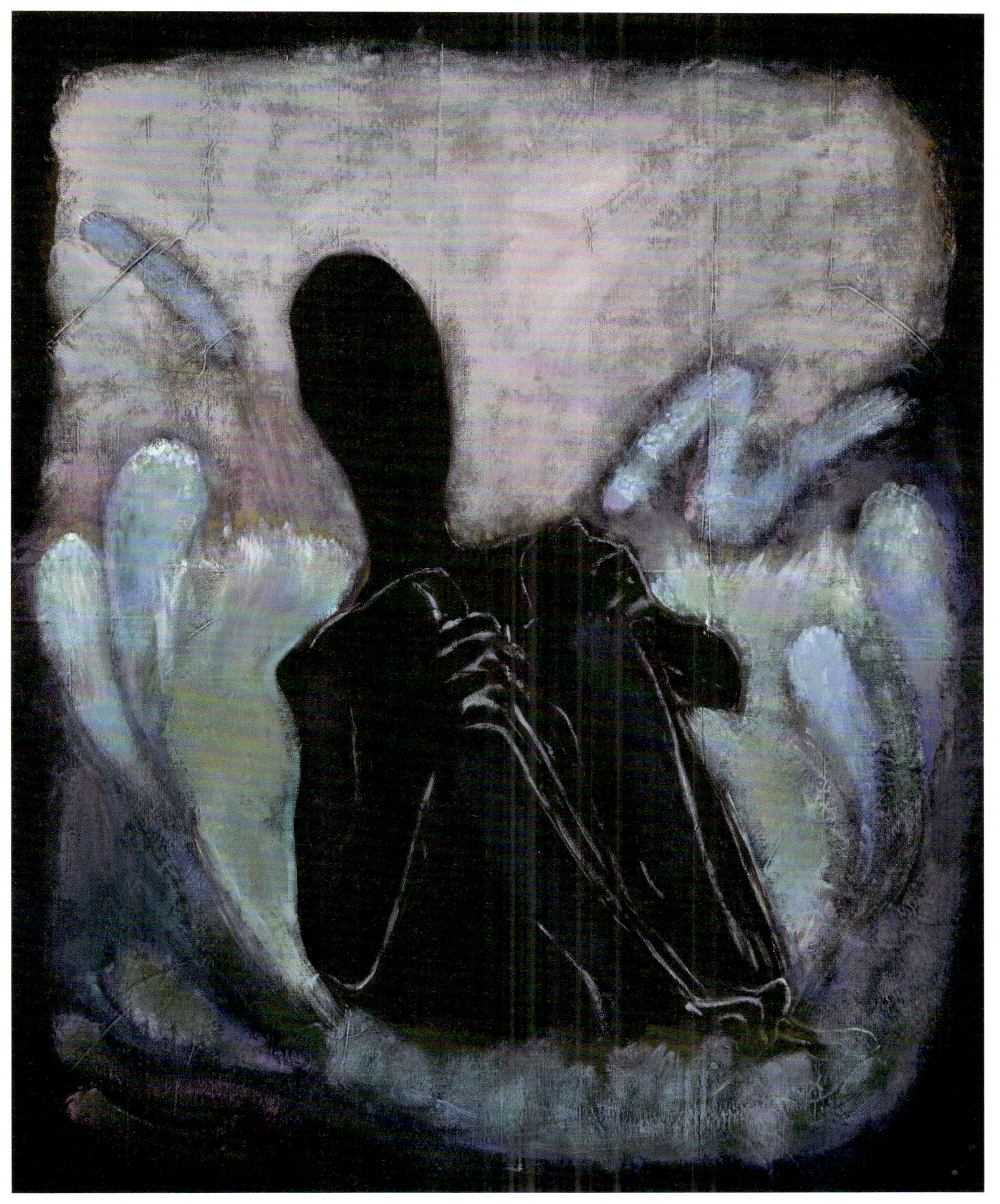

Wide, 2021
Acrylic and pastel on linen
63⅛ × 71⅛ in. (160.4 × 180.7 cm)

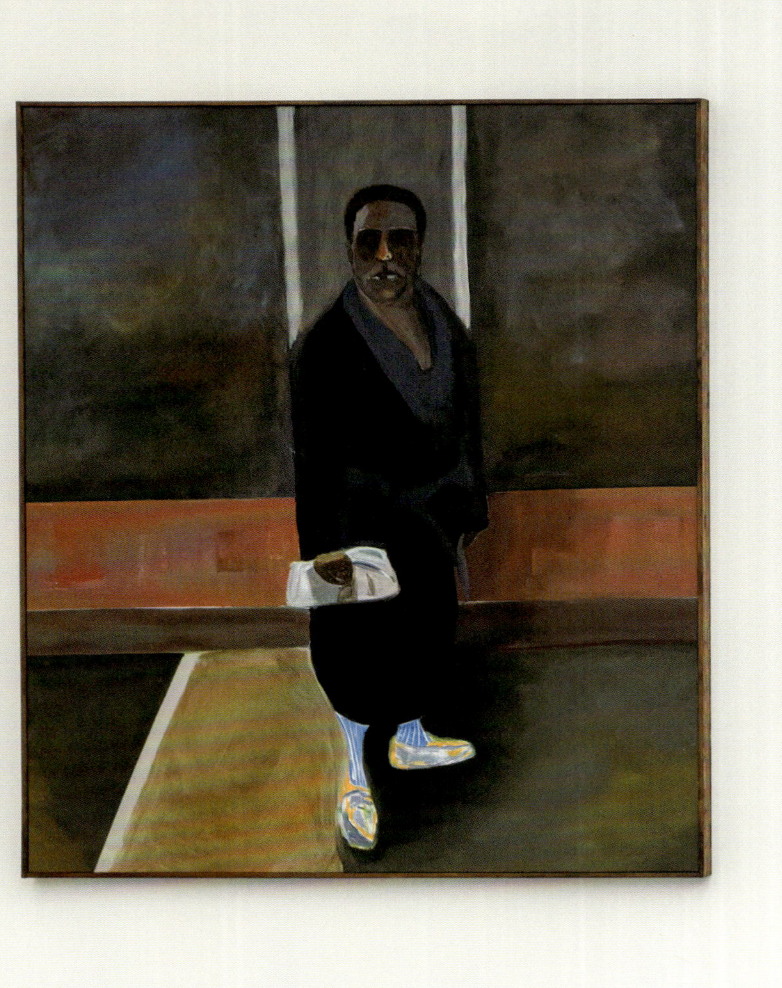
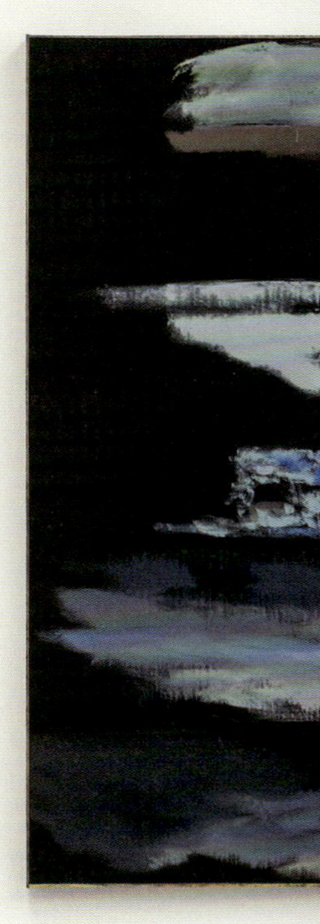

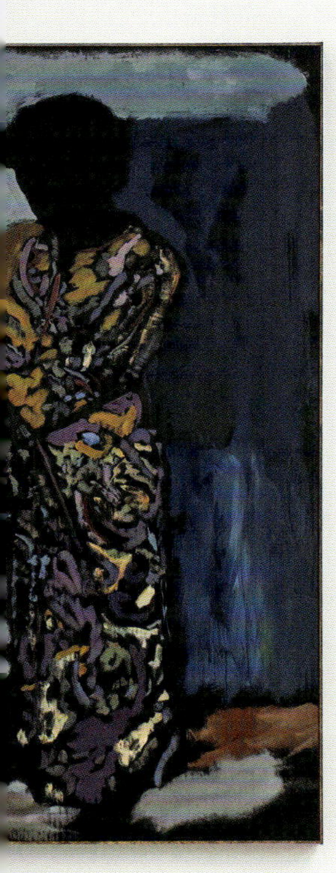
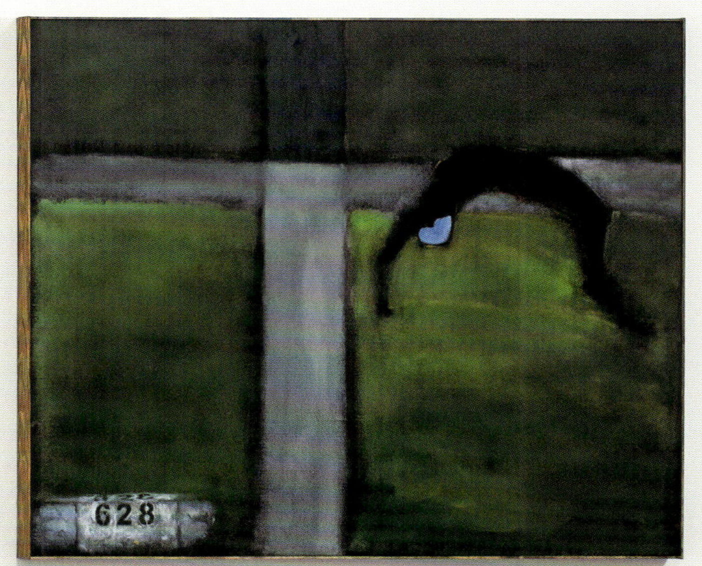

628

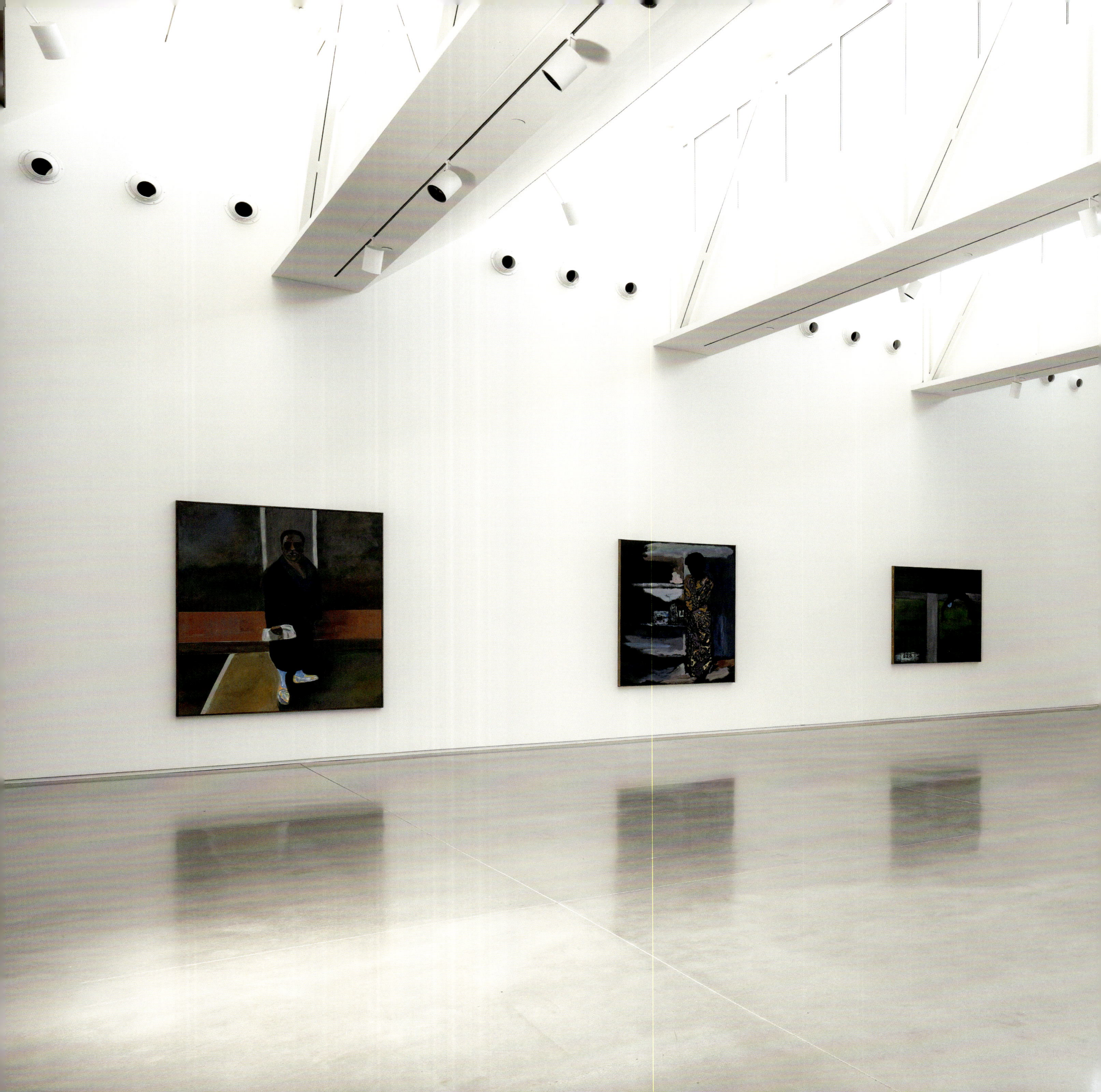

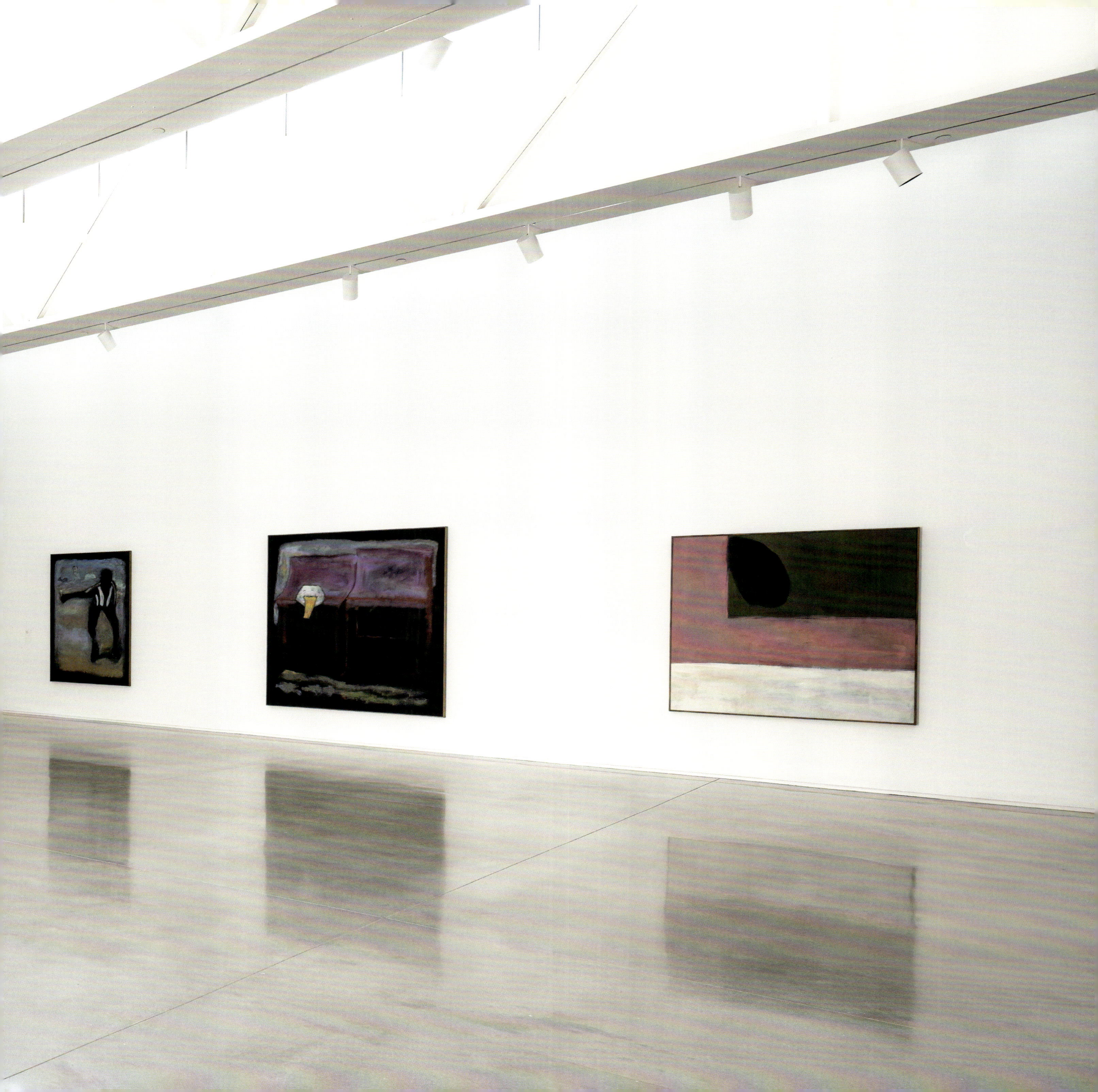

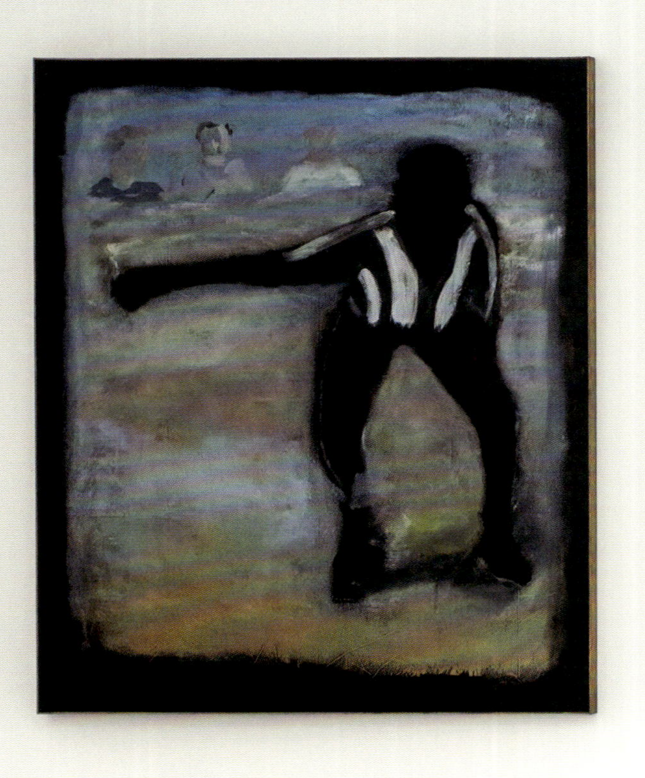
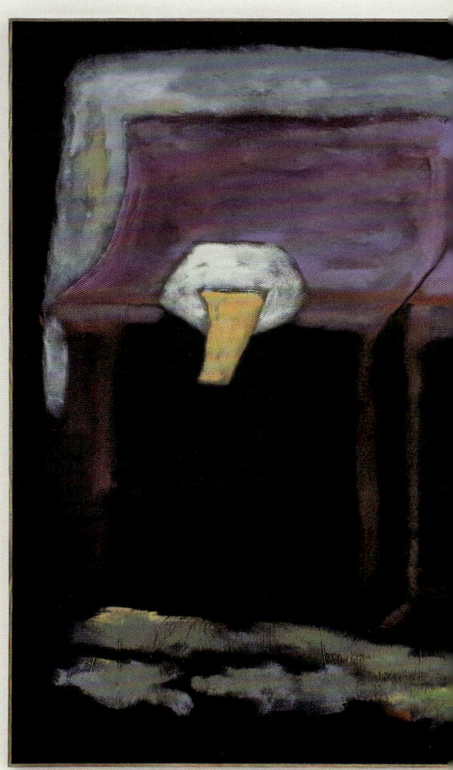

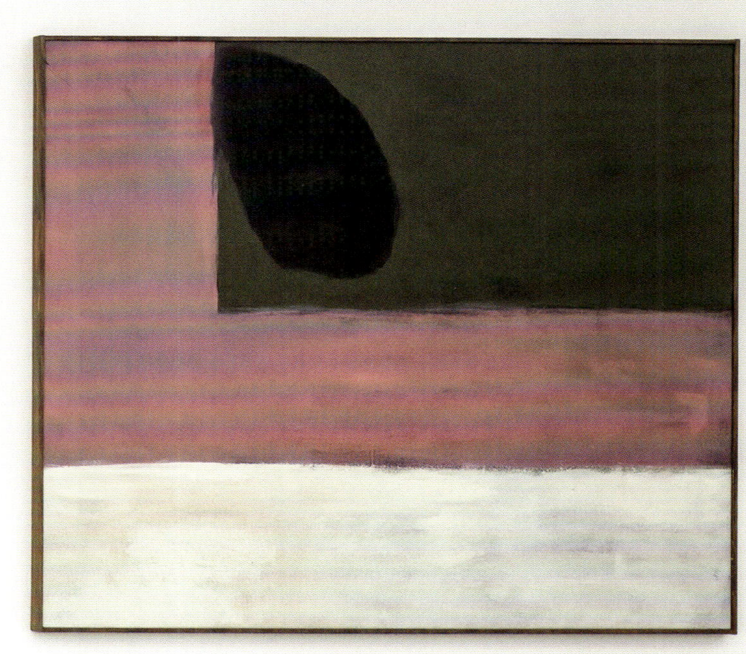

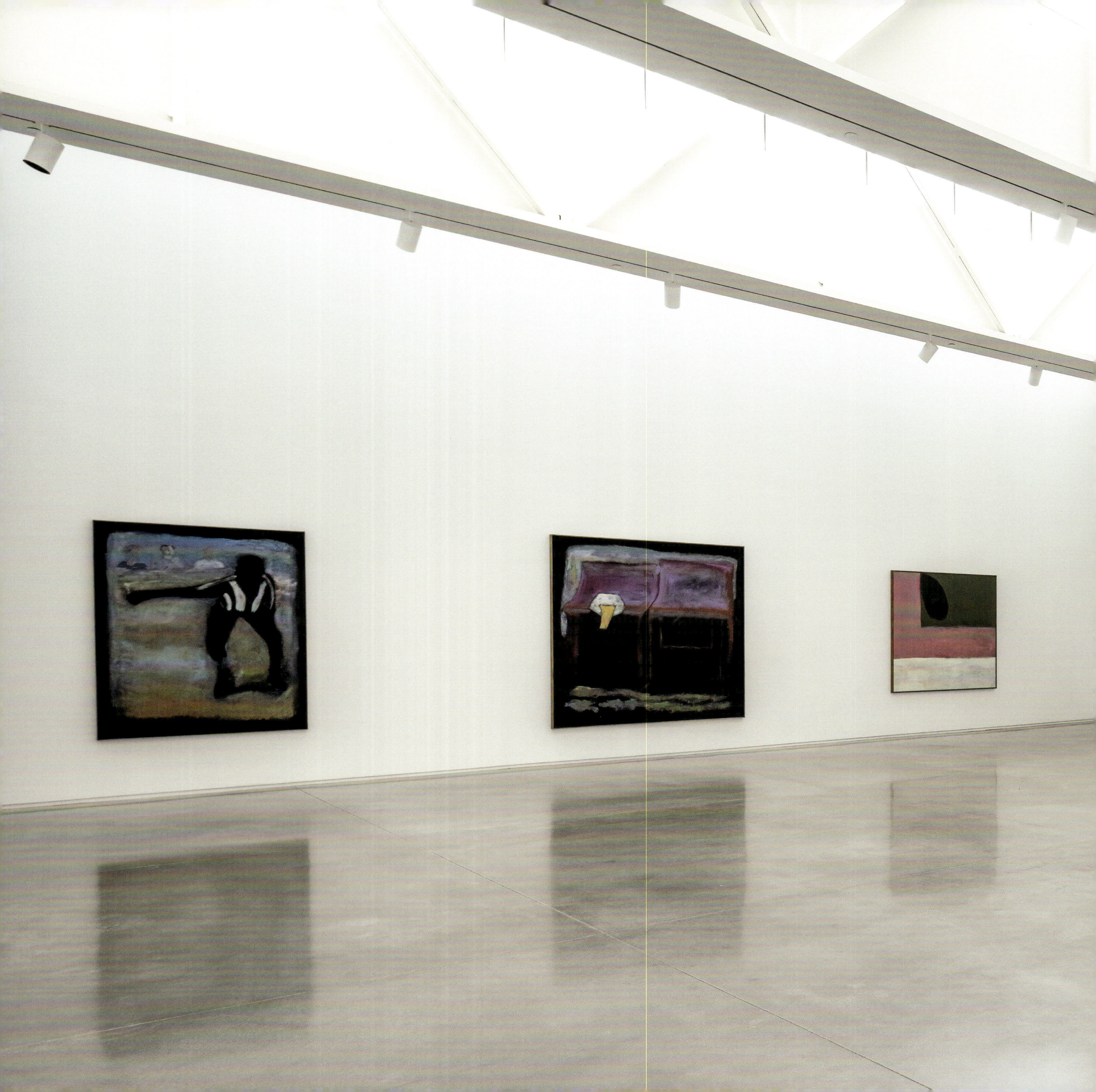

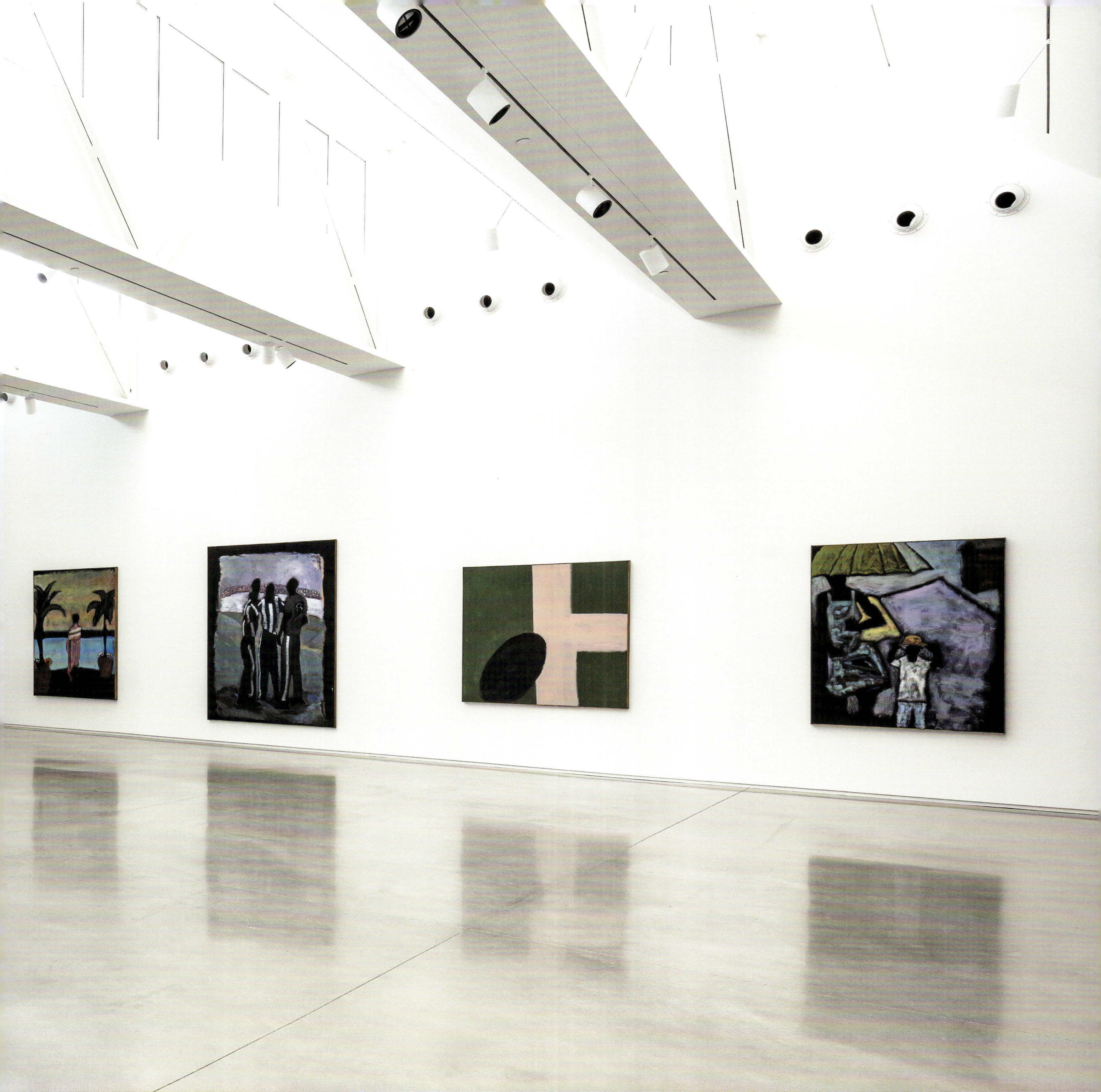

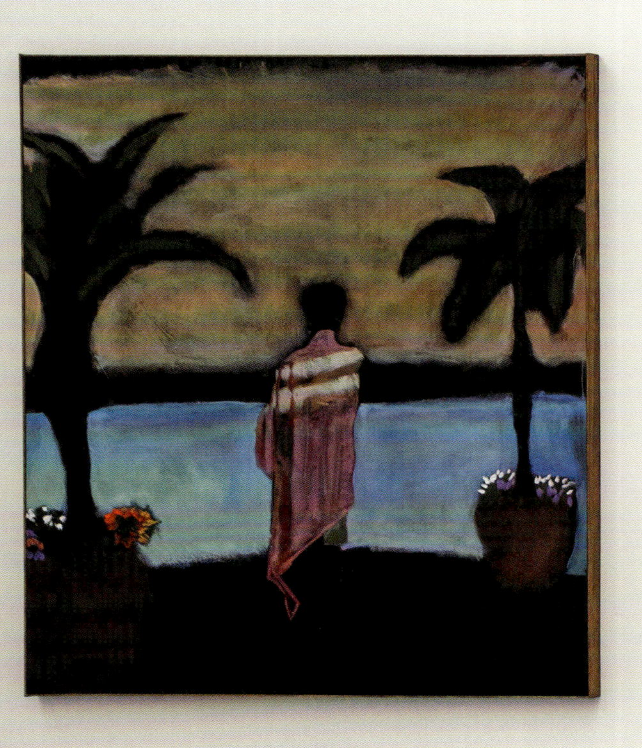
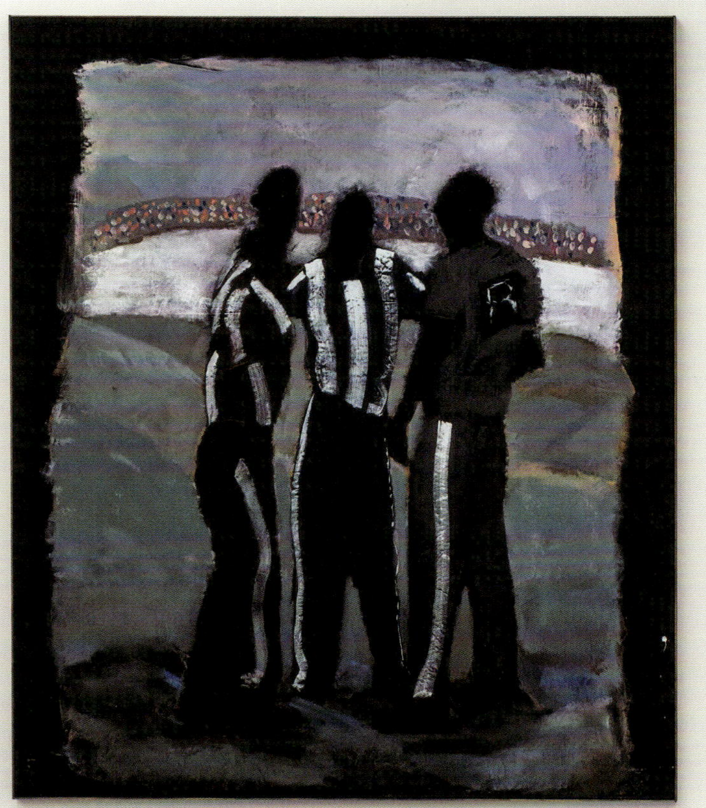

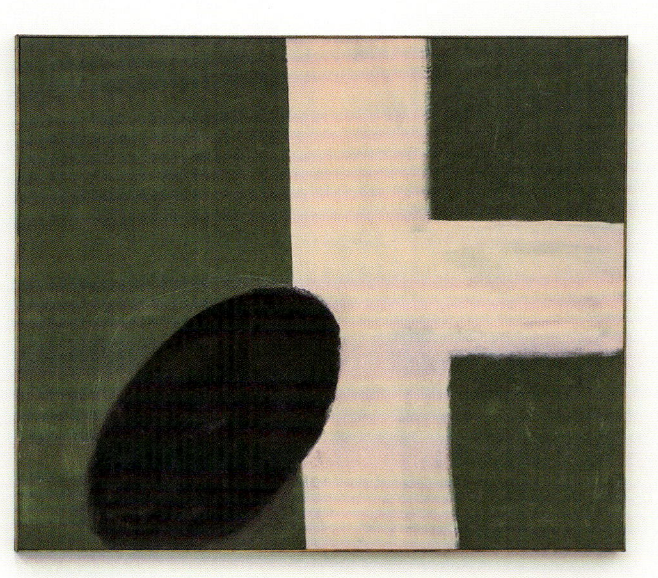
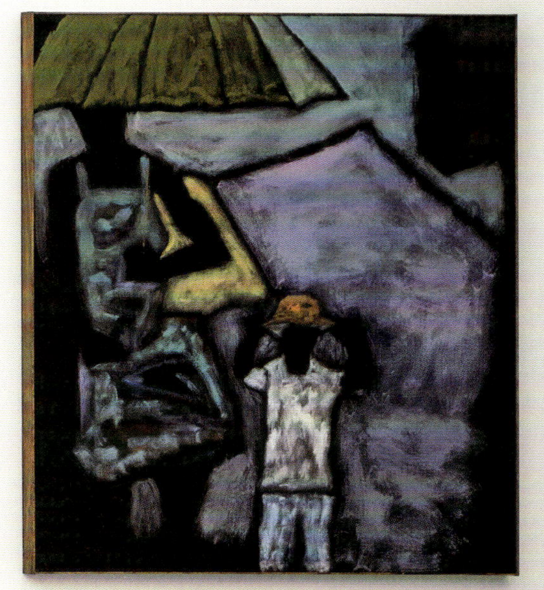

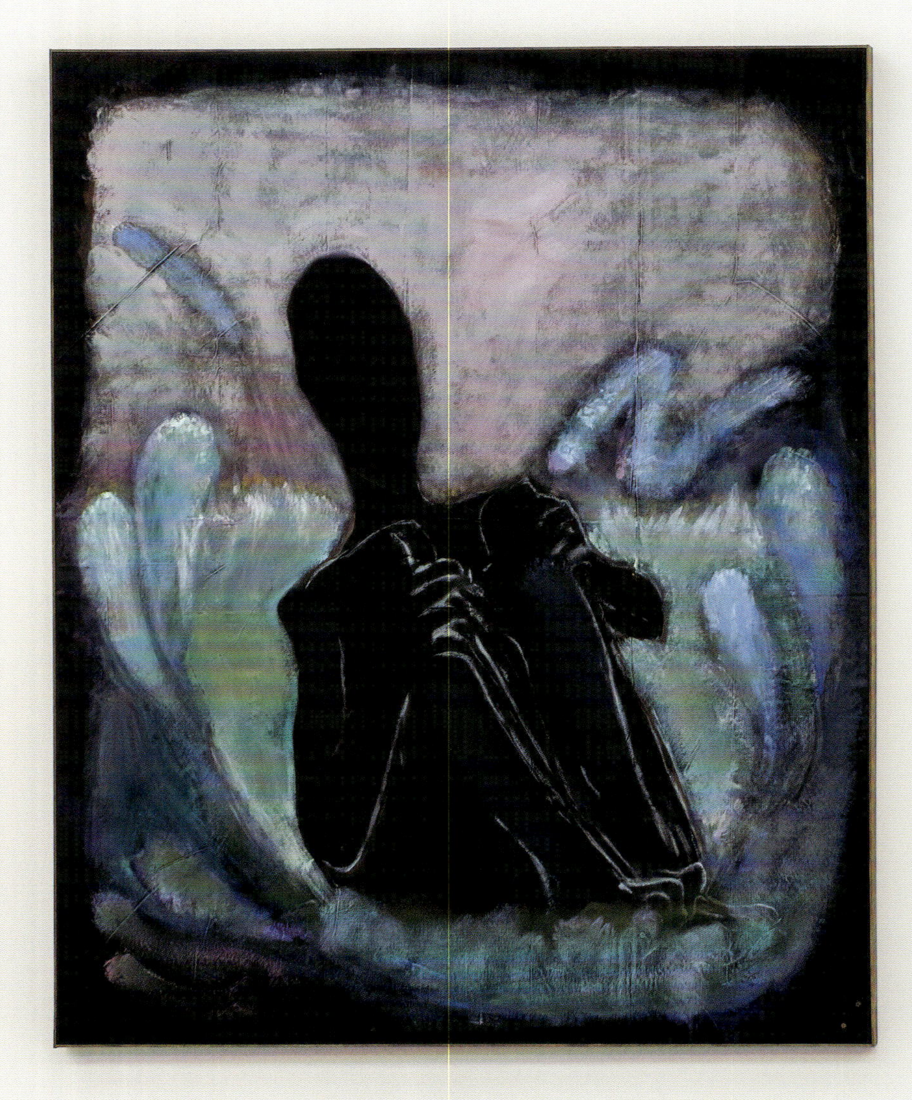

Published on the occasion of the exhibition

Reggie Burrows Hodges
Hawkeye

May 28–September 11, 2022

Center for Maine Contemporary Art
21 Winter Street
Rockland, Maine

© 2023 Center for Maine Contemporary Art

All works by Reggie Burrows Hodges
© Reggie Burrows Hodges

Design: Karma, New York
Installation photography: David Clough

Printed by Pureprint Group, Uckfield, England

Page 11, bottom: © 2023 Adolph and Esther
Gottlieb Foundation / Licensed by VAGA at
Artists Rights Society (ARS), New York
Page 16: © 2023 Salvador Dalí, Fundació
Gala-Salvador Dalí, Artists Rights Society

All rights reserved. No part of this publication may
be reproduced in any form or by any electronic
means without prior written permission from the
copyright holders.

ISBN 978-1-961883-00-0